# 100+
## School Exercises
## for Dressage

# 100+

## School Exercises for Dressage

### DEBBY LUSH

THE CROWOOD PRESS

First published in 2023 by
The Crowood Press Ltd
Ramsbury, Marlborough
Wiltshire SN8 2HR
enquiries@crowood.com

**www.crowood.com**

**British Library Cataloguing-in-Publication Data**
A catalogue record for this book is available from the British Library.

ISBN 978 0 7198 3503 2

**Dedication**
This book is dedicated to the memory of Mhairi McKay, a truly dedicated horsewoman, taken far too young, doing what she loved best – riding her precious horse.
Mhairi was unfailingly kind, supportive, and generous – someone who could invariably raise others' spirits with her ready smile and positive nature. Always keen to learn, she was about to embark on training to become a British Dressage judge alongside her riding career, but sadly it was not to be.
She is sorely missed by the eventing, dressage, and riding club communities of the Scottish Highlands – a true inspiration to so many.

Typeset by Chennai Publishing Services

Cover design by Blue Sunflower Creative

Printed and bound in India by Replika Press Pvt Ltd

# CONTENTS

## Counter-Canter Patterns

## More Advanced Therapeutic Lateral Work to Adjust Footfalls

## Developmental Exercises

## Exercises to Develop Engagement

## Exercises to Develop the Medium Gaits

## Exercises to Develop Half-Pass

## Exercises to Develop Walk Pirouettes

## First Steps Towards Flying Changes

## First Steps Towards Canter Pirouettes

## Warm-Down

## Advanced Exercises

## Exercises to Further Develop Engagement

## Patterns to Teach Flying Changes

## Developing the Canter Zigzag

## Patterns to Develop Canter Pirouettes

## PART 2: TRAINING STRATEGIES

## Sample Work Plans

## In Conclusion

# INTRODUCTION

Have you ever set out to school your horse and wondered why you are doing so, other than having been told that you should?

Do you ride into the school and wonder what to do, apart from going round and round in endless 20m circles?

It is little wonder that so many riders think that schooling is boring. If you do not understand *why* you are doing it, or how to make it interesting, then it is bound to feel like an aimless chore you are performing simply because you know that you should!

## WHY DO WE SCHOOL OUR HORSES?

The bottom line is that basic training (schooling) is **essential for a horse to lead a long, healthy, and happy working life.**

Even horses destined for pleasure riding, and not for the competition arena, need to be taught to respond calmly and with an understanding of the rider's aids. Start, stop, turn, go back, and move over, are all necessary basics for the purposes of manoeuvring safely along paths and through gateways. Trust is built between horse and rider by working together in a safe and controlled environment, such as a riding arena.

In addition, a basic physical training is essential for the horse's physical wellbeing:

- Healthy muscles – a logical, progressive schooling programme is what it takes to build the strength and fitness in the muscles to enable the horse to carry a rider while performing exercises of any variety, be it dressage, jumping, or simple hacking, without injuring himself.
- Joints – these need to be exercised to increase their flexibility and range, in order to perform ridden tasks without stress or damage.

- Skeleton, especially the spine – with the rider's weight sitting over the horse's spine, damage is highly likely to occur unless the core muscles that support the spine are strengthened.

The bonus to all this essential work is that a good education will also turn a horse into a comfortable and pleasurable ride.

If you do aim to train your horse further, to become a specialized sports horse developed to his maximum genetic potential, you will need a far greater comprehension of, and a much wider range of, the training tools available to advance his education.

This book offers you exercises ranging from the most basic, which should be used by every rider, through to advanced techniques for high-level competition horses.

## LEARNING HOW TO SCHOOL

Every horse begins life with his own individual strengths and weaknesses gifted by nature. In response to this, your training must first be:

1. Diagnostic – to discover and pinpoint those strengths and weaknesses, both mental and physical.

2. Therapeutic – respond with exercises targeted to address and overcome his weaknesses, and be able to use his strengths as reward for work well done.

3. Gymnastic – the development of his athleticism, once he has achieved the mental and physical status to be able to do so.

Once you gain an understanding of which exercises address these stages, and start using them in a targeted and responsive fashion, you will find schooling becomes far more rewarding. For example, if your horse is on the forehand, simply drilling school patterns will change nothing, but when you ride exercises designed to help the horse develop the weight-carrying capacity of his haunches, you will successfully lighten his forehand. Each exercise in this book will give you an insight into the reasons for its use, so that you can pick appropriately for your individual horse's issues.

---

## TIP

**Remember: a horse doesn't need to do what he *can* do – he needs to do what he *can't* do to progress.**

Schooling is a fascinating journey, and although you should set yourself an ultimate goal, you will never fully 'arrive' – there will always be more to learn. By turns thrilling and frustrating, done diligently and well, this journey becomes one of discovery and development, of growth and pleasure in the harmonious partnership you can develop with your horse.

---

## TRAINING TOOLS

Training a horse involves the combined use of aids and patterns; neither will do the job alone. While it is essential that you and your horse both understand the aiding system you have chosen to employ, without the use of a range of physical patterns your schooling will be dull, and your horse will never develop the flexibility and strength he needs for a long and healthy working life.

---

## DIFFERENT AIDING SYSTEMS

Did you know that there are different aiding systems? It is worth clarifying here that when we talk about aiding, there are a number of different schools of riding that teach different aiding systems to obtain the same result. There is no right or wrong – simply more than one legitimate training path. Horses trained in each of these systems can, and do, achieve the ultimate goal of Grand Prix, and perform at the

dizzy heights of World Championship and Olympic competition.

Generalized examples of schools would be: the Spanish Riding School-based systems, such as Germany and the UK employ, Iberian systems, the French school, and the Scandinavian. The most important consideration for a student must be that they ensure they learn only from trainers *working within one system*, and do not attempt to mix systems. This will only lead to confusion and as a result, stressed horses and riders.

## PATTERNS

*Patterns,* however, are universal – and that is largely what this book concentrates on. Where aiding is detailed as a means of riding a specific exercise, it is based on the Spanish Riding School system. If you need more clarity, you can find these aids covered in great detail in my previous book, *The Building Blocks of Training*, which is designed to lead you through the order in which exercises should be introduced to the horse.

Many of the patterns we use have been developed and refined over centuries of trial and error, with some of the movements we now classify as 'classical', and 'airs above the ground', having their origins in mounted combat. The length of time required to train a horse to such prowess meant that such animals were much valued and not easy to replace. Training methods that promoted longevity have stood the test of time, becoming what is now often termed 'classical training', but is, in fact, simply good training.

Some of the patterns in the latter part of this book are more recent innovations, based around educating horses to produce the movements required for the higher-level competition tests. All, however, are designed to enhance the horse's physical abilities, while at the same time maintaining his mental relaxation and acceptance of the rider's aids.

The horse's understanding of how to respond to the rider's aids (whichever aiding system you employ), will enable you to use a variety of patterns, each of which is designed to supple and/or strengthen various aspects of the horse's physique. Too many riders misunderstand the purpose of exercises, believing they need to train the horse to perform certain movements in order to compete at increasingly higher levels of dressage competition. In fact, the exercises are there to train and develop the horse's body, so that when the time comes to move up a level, the horse is already physically capable of the 'higher' movements, and all that is needed is refinement to the presentation, and the addition of more power. As such, many of the movements that riders believe to be too advanced for them to attempt should, in fact, be taught, albeit in an easier format, at much earlier stages of training than they appear in their completed state, in competition.

# TRAINING CHALLENGES

How far a horse can be taken, in terms of gymnastic and performance ability, depends on a number of factors at the outset.

- **Conformation** (the horse's physical structure) is a fundamental factor that cannot be changed by training, although a good knowledge of exercises targeted to address conformational weaknesses will mitigate this issue as far as is physically possible. Many of us find ourselves riding and training horses with far from ideal conformations, and these can be both more of a challenge, and more of a reward, when we are able to produce them to perform beyond expectation.

- **Movement** is largely pre-determined by conformation, but may also be influenced by experience (such as interaction with other horses), environment (hilly, challenging terrain during early physical development forms strong cartilage and healthy joints, whereas deep, muddy, or too flat ground may pre-dispose the horse to injury and limited movement), and, of course, training. The latter is responsible for enabling the horse to move his body and limbs under the foreign weight of a rider in such fashion that he does not injure himself, and is free to maximize his physical potential.

- **Temperament** is innate to the individual, though may be influenced to a degree by handling during upbringing. You cannot totally change a horse's temperament, but again, by logical, gradual, and kind training, you can channel it to become as close as possible to the desired outcome for a riding horse: attentive, willing, sensitive, and confident. If you have a horse with these attributes by nature the process is much easier, but such horses are highly sought after and, as a result, often expensive!

# USE THE SCALES OF TRAINING TO STRUCTURE YOUR SCHOOLING SESSION

If the basics of a horse's training are incorrect, or not well enough developed, nothing you attempt further along in his training will work – you need a solid foundation to build upon, which should be regularly revisited to ensure no faults have crept in unnoticed. Even with a Grand Prix dressage horse, riders will spend time working on the basics, because the ability to produce the higher, more exciting movements such as piaffe, passage, and canter pirouettes, depends upon solid, secure, and well-developed basics.

How do we know in which order to build this foundation?

We use the universally recognised SCALES OF TRAINING as our guide.

There are small variations in wording, but the most common list is:

1. Rhythm/relaxation
2. Suppleness
3. Contact
4. Impulsion
5. Straightness
6. Collection

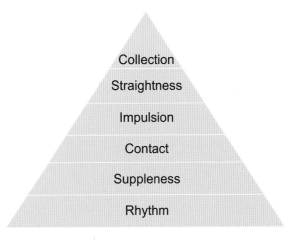

Plenty of riders can quote the scales, but fewer can put them in the correct order, which is knowledge critical to enabling you to use them!

The earlier scales – rhythm, suppleness, and contact – are relevant to all horses.

Competition horses should become confirmed in scales 1, 2, and 3, *plus* impulsion and straightness.

Higher-level horses must be accomplished in all six, and their riders will continually develop and refine them throughout their competitive life.

## How to use the scales in practice

Start every schooling session by assessing where the horse *is*, in relation to the scales. Run through them **in order** and note which scale is the first one that you feel is not satisfactory on that day. This will give you the focus of that day's training.

So, your first question will be: is the horse in a correct rhythm?

RHYTHM includes the clarity of the sequence of the gait, the regularity, and the tempo (speed of the rhythm).

If the rhythm is satisfactory for the horse's stage of training (rhythm will become more clearly defined as training progresses), then the next question is: is the horse supple?

SUPPLENESS should be both longitudinal (over the topline), and lateral (bending from side to side). Lateral bending should (eventually) become equal on both sides, but this is, of course, one of the biggest challenges when starting to train a horse, because horses are not born with two equal sides – their bodies will always curl in one direction or the other. Consequently, this is the most likely scale that will need attention for a long time to come.

Only with a relatively supple horse (particularly in regard to working with a rounded topline) should the rider worry overly much about the contact.

CONTACT is not solely about acceptance of the bit, but also about a willingness to step forward with the hind leg *up to* the bridle, and an understanding that *yielding to the bit will be rewarded by a yielding hand from the rider.* The acceptable amount of weight in the contact will vary from horse to horse, and from moment to moment, according to the balance, the exercise being ridden, and the training level of the horse. Contact is a huge subject all on its own.

When an acceptable contact (for that day) has been achieved, then, and only then, should the degree of impulsion be considered.

IMPULSION comprises four components:

1. the desire to go forward
2. the elasticity of the steps
3. the suppleness of the back
4. the engagement of the hindquarters

Notice how impossible this would be with a lack of suppleness. Too many riders, often as a result of a comment on their dressage test sheet, seek to solve a lack of impulsion by riding more aggressively, which results in greater speed. Unfortunately, speed *reduces* stride length and elasticity, rather than improving anything. Impulsion *cannot* be increased without the underlying building blocks in place: rhythm (including tempo), suppleness (which is destroyed by speed) and a good contact to provide the ability to direct impulsion into a useful asset.

STRAIGHTNESS is the trickiest scale to pin down, because it should be addressed on every horse as soon as it understands what the rider's aids mean. Straightness is essential to bring about the ambidexterity (equal use of both sides of the body) required for even loading of all four limbs, and hence even wear and tear on individual joints. It will not, however, be possible to fully achieve straightness without the preceding four scales in place, so focusing excessively on straightness without, for example, some degree of suppleness, would be counter-productive.

COLLECTION is the icing on the cake, only possible once the other scales are fairly well established, and yet although it is generally considered necessary only for higher-level competition horses, it is, in fact, the ultimate tool for preserving our horses. By nature, a horse takes sixty per cent of his weight on his relatively weak front limbs, and only forty per cent on his strong hindquarters. *Collection* gives him the physical strength and ability to transfer more weight to his rear end, and so reduce the weight carried by the more fragile front limbs, with the goal of preserving them more successfully. The added bonus comes with the delights offered by a light and mobile forehand – freedom of movement and true expression and beauty of the gaits.

# DRESSAGE TESTS AS A MEANS OF ASSESSING TRAINING

At first glance one might think that dressage tests are merely a sequence of movements strung together for the purpose of competition, but if you analyse them with more care you will start to appreciate that they are constructed with the specific goal of testing individual aspects of the horse's training.

In addition, by studying the progression of test demands up through the competition levels, it will also become clear that they are carefully designed with logical increases in difficulty.

Take, for example, the simple change:

1. At the lower levels, the simple change is generally positioned between two half 10m circles. This gives physical assistance to horse and rider with the preparation for the direct transitions, both down and up.

2. At the next level up, the simple change is required on either the short diagonal of the arena, whilst crossing the centre line, or on the half school line from E to B with the change taking place over X. With the downward transition taking place without the engaging assistance of a turn immediately preceding it, the horse must take weight back onto his haunches (collect) to achieve a good downward transition from the aids alone. On the other hand, the distance from the turn is still minimal, and so the horse is not as likely to have fallen onto his forehand by this point. The upwards transition is on a straight line, where the horse must go from the aids alone onto a named leg.

3. At more advanced levels, the simple change is requested on a long straight line, and sometimes out of counter canter. This requires a high degree of balance and engagement, and that the horse is totally on the aids for both transitions without any help from the pattern.

# WHY WE NEED A WIDE RANGE OF EXERCISES

To be successful as a trainer and rider, you should be in possession of multiple answers to any single problem. Different horses require different approaches; different physical issues need different exercises, and different mentalities require different handling. Having a large toolbox of exercises to choose from will mean you will have the ability to be successful with a wide variety of horse types – breed, conformation and temperament.

Using a broad selection of exercises keeps schooling more varied and less of a dull chore. Be flexible so that you can accommodate a horse's individual needs,

and keep training fresh and mentally engaging whilst pushing him physically as far as he is able to tolerate at that time.

As a horse develops, an exercise that was beneficial for a particular issue in the earlier stages might gradually lose effectiveness and need an upgrade to a new one. Remember: a horse does not need to do what he *can* do – he needs to do what he *cannot* do in order to progress, but always listen to him – once he becomes muscularly tired, there is no point continuing. Go out for a hack to cool off!

It takes many years to accumulate a catalogue of exercises, by learning from other trainers, and watching training given by those with more experience. The purpose of this book is to cover those basic exercises that everyone should know, and to offer (hopefully) some new ones, along with a description and an explanation of the training value of each pattern.

# HOW TO USE THIS BOOK

This book presumes you have a fair knowledge of the basic riding skills essential to effectively school a horse, and the ability to ride your horse in a functional, working outline. For greater depth in this area, you would benefit from studying my earlier book, *The Building Blocks of Training.*

By now, you should start to see why the accumulation of a vast range of exercises is essential for any trainer/rider, no matter what the age, level, or destiny of a horse might be. Successful trainers are always on the lookout for new exercises to add to their repertoire, and that is one of the main purposes of this book. What follows is by no means an exhaustive list of exercises, but outlines a mix of the essential basics, along with a few that will hopefully be new to you, to add to your catalogue.

## RESOLVE PROBLEMS THE LOGICAL WAY

If you have a problem with an exercise, the answer is *always* to return to a simpler related exercise, where you can re-confirm the basic work underlying the more challenging exercise. Only once the basic work becomes easy should you return to the more difficult exercise. You will find appropriate exercises suggested in the 'common faults' section of each pattern.

# EQUIPMENT

Most of the exercises described in this book are best performed in the confines of a dressage arena, although this may be as simple as a marked-out area in a field.

Some depend on the additional use of a fence, or a wall, on at least two sides alongside the track.

Many of the exercises can be ridden in both the 20m × 40m arena, and the 20m × 60m arena, although a few may be easier in one than the other. Where arena size is a factor in the success of a particular exercise, this is detailed in the text.

Some exercises involving poles are included, with a few offering the choice of substituting any sort of marker available, such as cones or barrels, if poles are not available.

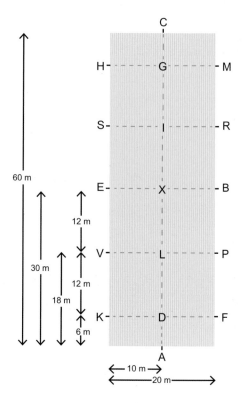

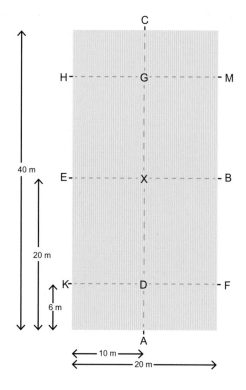

Note: When working with poles, always ensure there is someone with you for safety's sake.

Please note:

- **Where examples are given, the description is for one direction only.** The exercises can, and should be, ridden in both directions, unless targeted to the stiff or the hollow side of the horse, in which case this will be specified in the text.

- When a pronoun is required, I have used 'he' and 'him' to refer to the horse – this is done with no prejudice against mares, it is simply a stylistic choice for simplicity.

# PART 1

# PATTERNS AND EXERCISES

# FOUNDATION EXERCISES

These are the simple, basic exercises that should be taught to all horses, no matter what their purpose in life. They are designed to equip the horse with the mental understanding and the physical skills for a long and healthy career under saddle.

   The gait/s in which each exercise can be performed is detailed on each page.

## 1. 20m CIRCLE

**Walk, trot and canter.**

### Aims:

* 20m circles are the exercise you will use most throughout your training career.
* The required bend is gentle enough that all horses can accommodate it to some degree, even on their stiffer side.
* It is where you begin to equalise your horse's two sides.
* It is the basis of many other exercises.

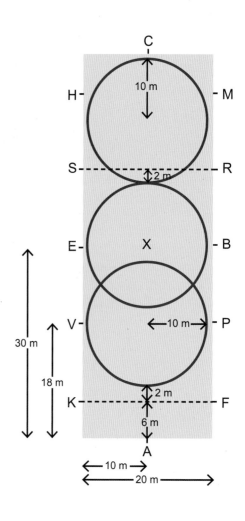

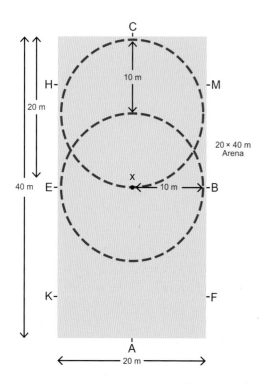

### How to:

1. On approach, prepare with small vibrations (half-halts) on the inside rein to develop a tiny inward

flexion at the poll, and to warn the horse you are about to leave the track.

2. To start, turn your shoulders so your outside hand travels slightly forward and inwards towards the crest, permitting some bend while keeping control of the outside shoulder. It also brings your inside hand slightly back without pulling backward.

3. Put more weight into your inside stirrup/seat bone.

4. Move your outside leg slightly back *from the hip* to control the hindquarters.

5. *To leave the circle*, straighten your shoulders and equalise the weight in both stirrups and seat bones.

## Common faults:

- *You struggle with the shape.* Learn the necessary touch points on the track and centre line (*see #2*). Place markers or poles as visual aids.

- *The horse falls in.* Press him out with your inside leg. *Do not* pull him outwards with the outside rein, which will compromise the bend.

- *He falls out.* Press the outside rein against his neck – your outside hand should have an inward/forward direction towards his inside ear – and use more outside leg.

- *He leans in like a bicycle.* Sit upright relative to the ground, and not to the horse. Push his ribcage out and up with your inside lower *and* upper leg.

- *He bends to the outside as you leave the circle.* This is caused by pulling on the outside rein in your effort to straighten. See above for how to leave the circle correctly.

## Combine with other exercises:

Many exercises can usefully be performed on the 20m circle, such as

- Transitions
- Spirals
- Satellite circles turning in, and out, of your 20m circle
- Lateral movements such as shoulder-in, and haunches-in

# 2. DIAMONDS TO IMPROVE 20m CIRCLES

Walk, trot and canter.

## Aims:

• To learn the points in the arena where circles should touch, to give you a true circle shape.

## How to:

1. In the 20m × 40m arena, put marks (paint, tape, or similar) onto your school fence at the appropriate points: halfway between E and the corner, at C, and halfway between the corner and B. *See* diagram.

2. Place a pole or cone just beyond X.

3. Now ride a diamond shape, going from one marker to the next in straight lines.

4. Once you can do this easily, start to ride curves between markers instead of straight lines, but make sure to touch each marker point.

5. When you can do this, you will be riding an accurate 20m circle.

6. Now repeat the exercise for the other positions within the arena where you will ride 20m circles, such as at E and B.

## Common faults:

• *The horse tries to drift outwards off your straight lines.* Keep more control of the outside shoulder with your outside rein pressed firmly against the outside of the horse's neck.

• *You lose the hindquarters to the outside in the turns.* Make sure your outside leg is drawn back into an outside leg position and pressed against his ribcage to keep control of the hindquarters.

• *The horse falls inward in the turns.* Use more inside leg to push his ribcage and shoulder out, especially as you straighten onto the line heading towards your next marker.

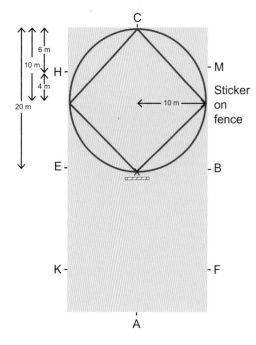

## TOP TIP

Once you can ride an accurate 20m circle, remember the feeling of how much you turned your shoulders to steer around it. When you want to ride a 20m circle in a different position in the school, use the same amount of upper body turn to produce the same size of circle.

# 3. 15m CIRCLES

**Walk, trot and canter.**

## Aims:

- This slightly smaller circle demands more body bend, and challenges the genuine control of the outside shoulder, and so, the correct tracking of the horse's hooves on the ground.
- Especially in canter, the reduced size, and hence, the increased arc in the horse's body, is one of the earliest exercises that will start to develop the engagement of the hind legs, and a small degree of collection.

## How to:

1. The aids are the same as for exercise #1, the 20m circle, but with a little more turn of your upper body to the inside.
2. 15m circles can be ridden in all the same positions within the arena as the 20m circle, but need more spatial awareness for accurate shapes. *See diagram, particularly noting that at C (or A) you must estimate 2.5m from the track both sides, and 5m away from X (short arena).*
3. The 15m circle ridden from one of the side markers, S, E, V, P, B or R goes to the opposite quarter line, also sometimes known at the three-quarter line.

## Common faults:

- *As for the 20m circle,* but with a greater percentage of the 15m circle ridden away from the track, the same faults may be more severe.
- *Learn the varied positions of this circle within the arena* so you become accustomed to noticing any deviations from size and shape, and use the corrections outlined in exercise #1.
- *Especially in canter, the horse may swing the hindquarters outwards* to avoid the engaging effect of the pattern. Keep a clear *outside leg position* and use it more firmly if need be.

## Combine with other exercises:

Ride a 15m circle at A or C to increase engagement prior to riding medium canter strides down the long side of the arena, and then ride another 15m circle at A or C immediately afterwards to aid recovery of balance and engagement before repeating.

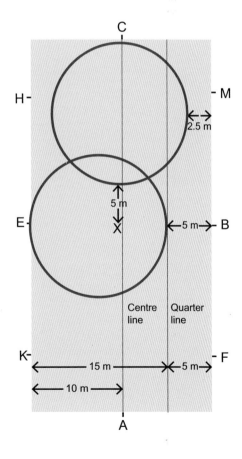

# 4. CHANGE THE REIN ACROSS THE DIAGONAL

**Walk and trot. In canter this requires a transition to trot before the end of the diagonal.**

## Aims:

- Frequent changes of rein are necessary because the horse must work in both directions to develop his muscles and balance.
- Always use the diagonal *after* the short side. Taking the turn *before* the short side is too sharp an angle for the horse to manage.
- There are various diagonals you can use, depending on the size of the arena:

### *20m × 40m arena:*

- Long diagonals, FXH and KXM
- Short diagonals, such as FE and KB

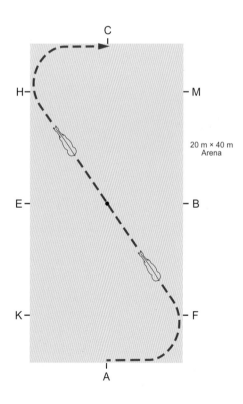

20 m × 40 m
Arena

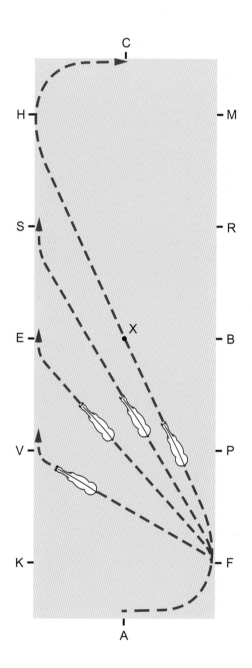

### 20m × 60m arena:

- Both of the above, but because of the extra length of the arena, the turns are all less sharp.
- Intermediate diagonals, such as HP and MV, and vice versa.
- Short diagonals, SP and VR.

### How to:

For example, the diagonal FXH.

1. Through the AF corner put a little more weight into your left stirrup and turn your upper body more towards the left.

2. Keep your outside rein firmly against the horse's right shoulder, and open your left rein to guide him into the turn.

3. Fix your eyes on the track one metre *before* H.

4. Change your diagonal three strides *before* arriving at the track, and not as you pass through X. Making the diagonal change in the centre of the line can cause loss of balance and straightness.

5. Reverse the above aiding as you approach H, and then ride into the corner.

### Common faults:

- *The horse falls to the outside at F.* Do not allow the neck to bend too much as you approach F, and press the outside rein more firmly against the shoulder.

- *The horse falls in at F.* Use a stronger inside leg to prevent his balance from going onto his inside shoulder.

### TOP TIP

Vary the patterns you use to change the rein – the diagonal, while very useful for a horse in the earlier stages of training, is the least demanding of patterns, and so less productive than patterns with more direct changes of bend, such as exercises #6, #7, #10, and #12.

# 5. THE HOURGLASS

**Walk and trot.**

## Aims:

- To introduce horses at an early stage of training to frequent changes of direction without demanding sudden changes of bend that might put them out of balance.

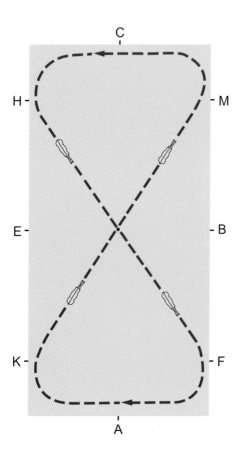

- Every change of direction challenges the horse's balance and coordination, so this exercise helps to develop both while keeping things simple.

## How to:

1. On the left rein, ride around the MCH short side in working trot rising, taking care not to go too deeply into the corners.
2. Turn across the HXF diagonal (*see #4*).
3. Just before F, change your diagonal.
4. Ride around the FAK short side.
5. Turn across the KXM diagonal.
6. Just before M, change your diagonal.
7. Repeat.

## Common faults:

- *The horse falls in, or falls out, on the corners.* Every corner is a portion of a small circle, so *see* exercise #1 for how to correct either issue.
- *The horse clings to the track instead of leaving it at the quarter marker.* Turn your body to look across the arena to where you are going, and put more weight into your inside stirrup, while closing the outside rein firmly against the horse's shoulder.

## Combine with other exercises:

When the horse's balance, both lateral and longitudinal, is more established, ride some lengthened strides on each diagonal, making sure to come back to regular length strides before the corners.

# 6. 2 × 20m HALF-CIRCLES

**Walk and trot. In canter, a change of lead is required over X.**

## Aims:

- A simple method of changing rein that can also be used to assess the equality of the horse's bend to the left and to the right.
- To teach a simple change of bend.
- Each time you change bend, you challenge the horse's balance and coordination, and if ridden correctly, improve both those aspects.

## How to:

1. In the 20m × 40m arena in rising trot, begin a 20m circle left (*see* exercise #1) from A.

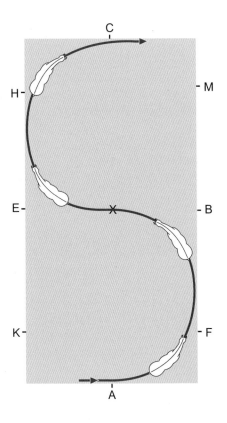

2. As you approach X, straighten until you are facing E. Aim to have three straight strides over the centre line – one before X, one over X, and one after.

3. One step *before* X, change your diagonal.

4. At X, step into the right stirrup and turn your shoulders towards the right to change direction onto a right rein 20m half-circle to finish at C.

## Common faults:

- *The bend to the two directions is unequal.* This is normal: horses, by nature, find it easier to bend one way than the other. Work on more full circles on the stiffer direction, making sure to encourage genuine bending around your inside leg.
- *The horse loses balance or becomes tense through the change of direction.* Ride the exercise at a slower pace and take care not to make the aid changes too suddenly.
- *The horse struggles with the change of bend.* Start asking for the bend change with the new inside leg (right, in this example) *before* X, so it is already in place before you make the change of direction.

## Combine with other exercises:

In canter, change the lead through trot over X.

---

### TOP TIP

Use this pattern frequently as a method of changing rein, rather than going across the diagonal of the school.

# 7. 2 × 10m HALF-CIRCLES

**Walk and trot. In canter, a change of lead is required over X.**

## Aims:

- To change the rein.
- To challenge and improve the horse's bend and balance.
- At a later stage, ridden in canter, this is the ideal introductory pattern for riding a simple change of lead.

## How to:

1. For example, in walk on the right rein, begin a right 10m half-circle at B.
2. As you approach X, begin to straighten the horse.
3. Ride straight for one stride over X.
4. In the stride after X, put more weight into your left seat bone and stirrup.
5. Turn your shoulders to the left, and ask for left bend by squeezing with your left leg and vibrating the left rein.
6. Begin a left 10m half-circle.
7. When you arrive at the track at E, straighten your shoulders and ride on down the track.

## Common faults:

- *The horse falls either in or out on one of the half-circles.* Review the corrections described for these faults in exercise #1.
- *The horse is not straight through X.* Take your time through the change of direction: your goal is to ride approximately three straight strides in the middle of this exercise – the last stride before X is where you are straightening, as you ride through X the horse is totally straight, in the stride after X you are beginning the new bend but still travelling in a straight line.
- *The two half circles are not the same size.* Practise riding a full 10m circle at B several times before changing direction, then practise riding several full 10m circles starting at X and ending at E. Once you can do this, simply ride the same lines when you ride the half-circles. Place markers at the peak of each half-circle as a visual cue.

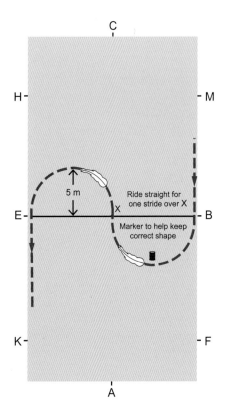

## TOP TIP

Ride the first half-circle a little deep, so that you arrive on the centre line *slightly* before X, and then ensure you get three straight strides before turning away into the new direction.

# 8. SHALLOW LOOPS IN TROT

## Aims:

- Developing balance and coordination by asking for two mild changes of bend over the length of one long side of the arena.
- A good warm-up exercise, particularly for a young horse.
- A loop is another name for a shallow serpentine.

## How to:

1. Decide the depth of your loop: anything between 3m and 10m.
2. For example, a 10m loop in the 20m × 40m arena, ridden on the KEH long side, on the right rein.
3. If you struggle to visualise the shape, put a cone or other marker 9m in front of E.
4. Come out of the AK corner with a right bend, and head towards X. About halfway to X, start to ask for a left bend.
5. As you approach X, begin a gentle left-hand curve. If you have placed a marker, keep it on your left.
6. As you leave X, you should be heading towards H.
7. Halfway between X and H, develop a right bend, which you will keep as you go into the HC corner.

You do not need to change diagonal with each change of bend, although you may find it more comfortable to do so, particularly on deeper loops.

You can also ride loops from, for example, quarter line to quarter line, or simply a few metres either side of the centre line.

moves his ribcage away from each leg in turn. In the example above, first the right leg, then the left leg, then the right leg. If he ignores one of your legs, try riding a turn around the forehand (#19) to reinforce the correct bending response to your leg, before returning to this pattern.

## Common faults:

- *Poorly shaped figure.* Remember to make the line last for the entire long side; do not return too sharply after the midpoint.
- *Struggling to achieve the bend changes.* The horse will naturally be more difficult to bend in one direction. Insist as firmly as you can that the horse

> **TOP TIP**
>
> Make sure to turn your upper body clearly towards the new direction each time you change the bend.

# 9. TURN ACROSS THE SCHOOL TO CHANGE REIN

**Walk and trot. In canter, a change of lead is required over X.**

### Aims:

- To change the rein in a shorter distance than when using the diagonals of the arena.
- In the 20m × 40m arena: from either E to B (known as the 'half school'), or vice versa.

- In the 20m × 60m arena this can also be done from S to R, and from V to P (and vice versa).

### How to:

1. The physical actions are identical to those described in 'Change the rein across the diagonal' (#4), although the turn away from the track is a full 90 degrees, as opposed to the shallower turns onto the various diagonals.

### Common faults:

- *See exercise #4 for the most common faults.*
- *Over-turning may be a problem with this line.* Make sure to fix your eyes on the letter you are heading towards, and to straighten up promptly from the turn, using the outside rein to straighten the neck and bring the horse's shoulders into alignment. The turn will take around three strides to accomplish, so start straightening up after the first two steps.

### Combine with other exercises:

- Add in a trot-walk-trot transition over the centre line. Make the downward transition two steps before the centre line, walk for three to four steps before returning to trot and preparing for the turn to the new direction.
- In canter, ride a canter-trot-canter transition in the same manner as the trot-walk-trot described above, but to include a change of canter lead.
- At a more advanced training stage, ride a simple change: canter-walk-canter, in the same position as above.

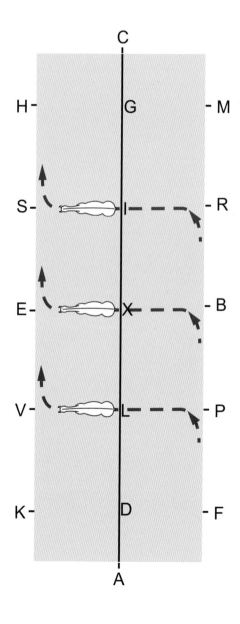

# 10. HALF-CIRCLE AND RETURN TO THE TRACK (JUG HANDLE)

Walk and trot. In canter, this requires either a transition to trot upon returning to the track, (with or without a following strike off to the opposite canter lead), or proceeding in counter canter (*see #41*).

## Aims:

- To change the rein using a half-circle of a size appropriate to the horse's level of suppleness.
- Traditionally, this pattern is performed with the half-circle first, followed by the straight line (incline) back to the track, but can also be ridden in the opposite direction for variety.

## How to:

1. Near to the end of one long side, begin a circle. This will usually be of 15m or 10m, but can be anything in between.

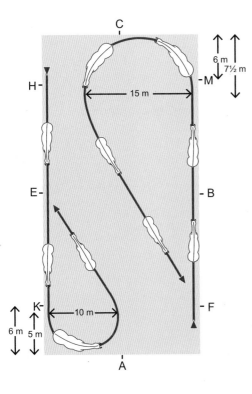

2. Halfway round the circle, straighten onto a straight line – an incline – heading back towards a point of your choosing on the track, to arrive on the other rein.

3. In rising trot, change the diagonal two or three strides before arriving at the track.

4. If done in canter with the intention of maintaining counter-canter, make the half-circle as small as the horse can manage without losing canter quality, so that the incline return is as shallow as possible to assist maintenance of balance.

## Common faults:

- *Falling in or out on the half-circle.* Use the corrections for this fault as described for the full circle (#1).
- *Making the incline in the wrong direction.* Remember your goal is to arrive on the opposite rein – the incline is simply a short diagonal.

## Combine with other exercises:

Use this method of changing the rein for variety.

Capitalize on the engaging effect of a small circle, and use it to set up some medium trot steps on the incline.

# 11. CENTRE LINES

**Walk, trot and canter, although if making a change of direction, canter will require a change of lead at some point.**

## Aims:

- Centre lines can be ridden with or without a change of direction, and in both directions, A to C, and C to A.
- An excellent way of checking the horse's straightness.
- They appear in every dressage test, so useful to practise!

## How to:

1. Starting on the right rein, as you travel through the corner preceding A, ask for a little more right bend, and put more weight into your right seat bone and stirrup.

2. Two to three strides *before* A, turn your shoulders to begin turning onto the centre line.

3. As soon as you have left the track, straighten your shoulders to start straightening the horse.

4. Fix your eyes on C and without hurrying, ride positively towards the letter.

5. Three or four strides before you arrive at C, start asking for a mild bend to the direction in which you intend to turn.

6. If you are changing rein in rising trot, this is also the moment to change your diagonal.

7. Two to three strides before C, turn your shoulders to start your turn onto the track.

8. Ride into the following corner.

## Common faults:

- *Overshooting A.* Start your turn a step or two earlier, and keep a firmer outside rein to control the outside shoulder.
- *Undershooting A.* Ride with a stronger inside leg to keep the horse upright and prevent him falling in.
- *The centre line is not straight.* Remember to keep your eyes on C and ride straight at the letter.
- *The horse falls in or out at C.* This turn is basically a half-10m circle, so review corrections described in exercise #1.

## TOP TIP

- Ride your turns at either end as if you were riding 10m half-circles – this gives a smoother appearance to the pattern.
- Never try to make corrections to a wiggly centre line, as this will cause more deviations. Instead, to make it straighter, ride more positively forward towards C.

# 12. THREE- AND FOUR-LOOP SERPENTINES

Walk and trot. In canter, a change of lead is required at each crossing of the centre line, unless counter canter is chosen.

## Aims:

- Each change of direction challenges the horse's balance and coordination.
- To test and develop suppleness.
- To promote relaxation.
- Four-loop serpentines are a method of changing rein.
- Serpentines are the basic building block for other exercises that eventually culminate in the Grand Prix zigzag.

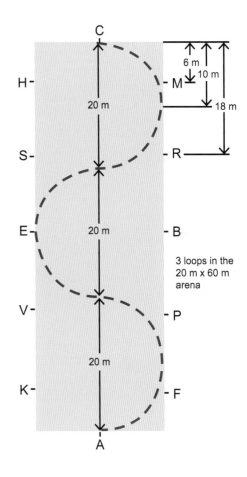

3 loops in the 20 m x 60 m arena

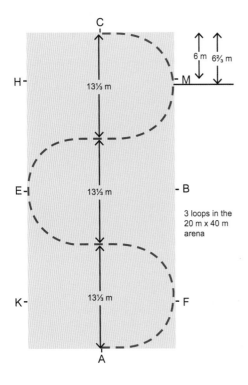

3 loops in the 20 m x 40 m arena

## How to:

1. Learn to parse the arena into equal parts – *see* diagrams for distribution.
2. Start your first loop as if you were riding a circle.
3. As you approach the change of direction, begin to straighten your horse.

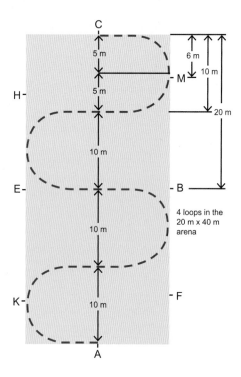

4 loops in the
20 m x 40 m
arena

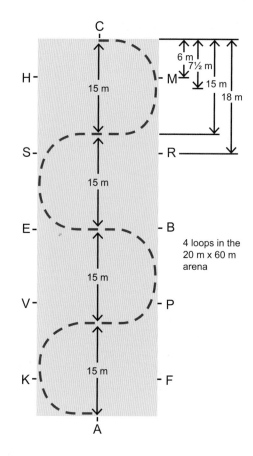

4 loops in the
20 m x 60 m
arena

4. In rising trot, change your diagonal one step **before** the centre line – this warns the horse that you are about to change direction.

5. As you cross the centre line, apply your new inside leg to initiate the new bend.

6. In the next stride, turn your shoulders towards the new direction and start the new curve.

7. To develop accuracy, position markers as touch points on the track, and also just inside the peak of each loop.

## Common faults:

- *Your horse does not bend well, or at all, in one direction.* Try putting a circle into the peak of the loop on the stiff side, so you can fully establish the bend before continuing with the figure (*see #13*).

- *He falls in on one bend, and out on the other.* Try keeping him straighter through the entire exercise – only allow a small degree of bend to either side.

## Combine with other exercises:

- Add transitions either side of the centre line: transition to walk before the direction change, and back to trot just after (#15).

- Use serpentines with a young or hot horse, to relax him between sections of canter work – frequent changes of direction will take his mind off a return to canter.

## TOP TIP

Focus on making the changes of direction gradual, over at least three strides. Until he is well balanced and flexible, do not make the changes of bend and direction in the same stride.

# 13. SERPENTINE WITH CIRCLES IN THE PEAKS OF THE LOOPS

Walk and trot.

## Aims:

- To further develop correct and equal bending in both directions.
- To improve balance during the frequent changes of bend required by a serpentine.

## How to:

1. The simplest form of this exercise is the four-loop serpentine in the 20m × 60m arena, because each loop consists of a 15m half-circle connected by a straight section across the centre line (*see #12*).

2. In the 60m arena, start a four-loop serpentine.

3. In the peak of each loop, starting from the point where the loop touches the track, ride a full 15m circle before resuming the serpentine.

## Common faults:

- *The horse falls either in, or out, on the circles.* Review the corrections for dealing with these faults detailed in exercise #1.
- *The horse finds the change of direction easier one way than the other.* Review exercise #6 for how to improve the ease when changing direction.

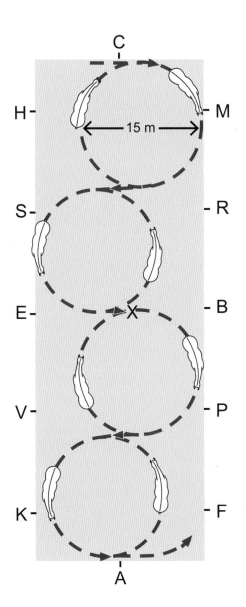

## TOP TIP

Ride more than one circle on the horse's stiffer rein, and do not continue with the serpentine until you are satisfied with the bend in that direction. Alternatively, *only* ride the circles on the stiffer rein: so, in other words, ride a normal serpentine loop on the more supple side, and put a circle into the loop on the stiffer side.

This is a pleasing pattern to include in a Novice Freestyle dressage test where 15m trot circles are a compulsory movement.

# 14. TROT-WALK-TROT, WITH COUNTED STEPS OF WALK

## Aims:

- To improve reactions.
- Increase activity and engagement of the hindquarters.
- Learn how much preparation is needed to position transitions precisely within the arena.

This is a keystone exercise required in many of the earlier dressage tests, and out of which the half-halt will develop. At the very highest level these transitions are the basis for piaffe.

## How to:

1. These can be performed on the long side, the short side, in corners, on the centre line, and between turns across the arena.

2. Decide beforehand how many steps of walk you require. If you are practising a dressage test, the sheet will specify. Common numbers are: 2 to 4, 3 to 5, or 3 to 7.

3. In working trot, prepare a downward transition by sitting still in the saddle, draw both your lower legs *slightly* back and close them, and make small vibrations on both reins with your fingers to move the bit softly in his mouth.

4. Once he steps under behind, relax your aids to allow him to drop into walk.

5. Count the number of steps by *counting each front footfall.*

6. Ask for trot when you are a couple of steps short of the final required number.

7. You should be in trot before the count runs out.

## Common faults:

- *The horse overshoots the prescribed position in the arena.* Start asking for the downward transition earlier.

- *The horse takes a long time to respond to the request for trot.* Repeat once with sharper leg aids, and/or back up your leg with your stick.

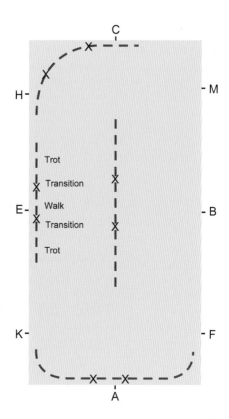

- *The horse jogs, or is unsettled in the walk.* Make sure you relax your legs during the walk – do not push the walk with your lower leg, use your seat instead.

## TOP TIP

If your horse is tense in the walk steps, then stay in walk until he relaxes before returning to the trot. While this will not be possible in a test, in training always take as much time as you need to help him lose his anxiety or anticipation. This will pay off in the long term.

# 15. SERPENTINE WITH WALK/TROT TRANSITIONS OVER THE CENTRE LINE

### Aims:

- To give the horse time to find balance through the changes of direction.
- To set up for the future the half-halts that will eventually replace the full transitions.

### How to:

1. Start a serpentine, either three or four loops.
2. As you leave the track, use a small half-halt (*gently squeeze the outside rein*) to warn the horse you are going to make a transition.
3. Just before the centre line, make a transition to walk.

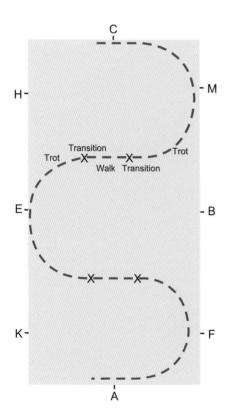

4. During the walk, change your aids and the horse's position towards the new bend ready for the next loop.
5. Just after the centre line, ride a transition to trot.
6. Continue around the next loop and repeat.

### Common faults:

- *The downward transition is late, possibly even after the centre line.* Next time, prepare earlier, and/or ask for the transition sooner.
- *There is resistance to the bend change.* Ensure you not only change your leg and hand aids, but also your weight in the saddle so that it is towards the new direction. If your weight remains to the old direction, you will pull the horse onto his outside shoulder and make it hard for him to remain in balance.
- *The change of bend takes a long time.* Initially, do not worry about this – allow the horse to take time to achieve the bend change. If you only have a few steps of trot before the next transition to walk, that does not matter: it is more important that the horse changes bend and maintains balance so that with practice he will get quicker about it instead of being worried.

---

### TOP TIP

Once this exercise becomes easy (and it is not as easy as it sounds!), gradually reduce the number of walk steps between the transitions until you can dispense with them altogether, simply performing a half-halt before the change of bend.

# 16. CHANGE OF CANTER LEAD ON THE DIAGONAL

## Aims:

- To check that the horse understands the canter aids for both leads.
- To teach the horse to strike off into both canter leads with ease.
- This is one of the simplest places in the arena to help an inexperienced or unbalanced horse to strike off on a 'sticky' canter lead.

## How to:

1. Start this exercise on the horse's easier canter lead – in this example, left lead.

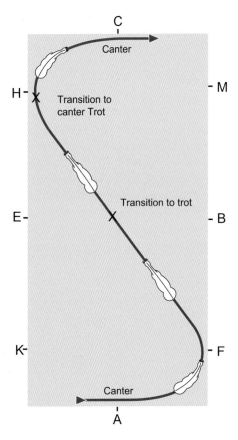

2. Establish left-lead canter.
3. Turn across the FXH diagonal.
4. Just after X, return to trot.
5. Re-balance the trot as quickly as possible.
6. At H, ask for right-lead canter.
7. Establish canter fully before repeating the pattern in the opposite direction.

## Common faults:

- *The horse loses balance to trot.* Do not worry too much at this stage – a small lack of balance may help with getting the new canter lead strike off! If there is no issue with striking off on the correct leg, then make the downward transition slightly earlier, and take more time to re-balance before the corner.

- *The horse picks up the wrong canter lead.* Return to trot, change the rein in trot, and pick up the original canter lead before repeating the exercise. Make sure when you ask for the new canter that your weight is clearly in the inside stirrup.

- *The horse struggles to pick up canter.* Using a short whip, tap him on the inside shoulder as you ask for canter. In the earlier stages of training this can be a great help to the horse to understand which front leg should be leading in canter.

## Combine with other exercises:

Use this as another method of changing the rein. It is particularly useful with a horse that struggles to strike off on one canter lead.

# 17. SPIRALS

**Walk, trot and canter.**

## Aims:

A multi-purpose exercise to:

- Develop suppleness.
- Teach leg yield.
- Increase engagement.
- Connect the horse from inside leg to outside rein.
- As a preparation for transitions, or for an advanced horse, working canter pirouettes.

## How to:

1. Ride a 20m circle at E.
2. Gradually decrease the circle around X.
3. Go down to the smallest size circle the horse can manage without losing rhythm or impulsion.
4. Stay there for one or two rounds.

5. Gradually increase the circle, unwinding it *as gradually as you reduced it.*
6. Proceed to your next exercise, or repeat.

## Common faults:

- *The spiral does not remain centred around X.* Place a marker on X to use as a visual reference.
- *The horse does not move inward easily.* Use your outside aids – outside rein against the neck, and outside leg, to shepherd him in. Exaggerate your upper body turn to the inside, open the inside rein, and put more weight in the inside stirrup.
- *The horse rushes outwards, arriving back on the large circle within a few strides.* Keep a firm outside rein against his neck, and ride more forwards than sideways. You may need to use some outside leg. Aim to take at least one full circuit, preferably two, to return to the 20m circle.

## Combine with other exercises:

Use spirals to set up canter transitions. The inside hind leg will be in the perfect position underneath the horse to lift his body weight, rather than using his front legs to drag himself into canter.

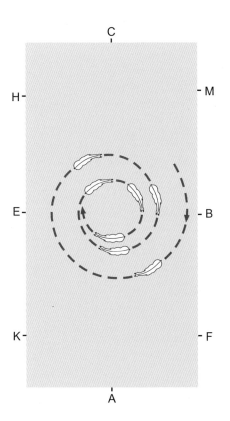

## TOP TIP

One of the goals of the spiral is to achieve a clear inside leg to outside rein connection. Once you have returned to the 20m circle, check this out by yielding the inside rein forward for two steps – if you have a true connection, the horse's bend will remain unchanged.

When you leave a spiral, keep the feeling that you are still pushing the horse outward, even as you travel along a straight line. This will sustain the inside leg to outside rein connection.

# 18. LEGS ON SHORT SIDE, LEGS OFF ON LONG SIDE

**Walk, trot and canter.**

## Aims:

- To teach a non-forward-thinking horse that it is *his* responsibility to maintain impulsion without the necessity for frequent leg aids.
- To improve reaction to your leg aids by *only* using your legs when you want him to do something different.

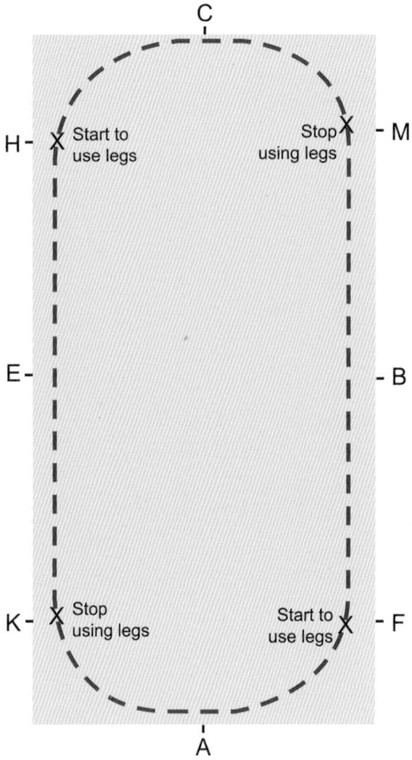

## How to:

1. In your chosen gait, ride large around the arena (on the right rein in this example).
2. On the short side, apply leg aids to bend the horse in the corners, and to increase impulsion.
3. On the long sides, *DO NOT* use your legs. Keep them relaxed and hanging loosely.
4. If there is a loss of impulsion, or a break to a slower gait, use your schooling whip to keep him going. If he is particularly stubborn, use one over-large leg aid along with the stick to startle him forward, but then cease using the legs again until you get to the next short side.
5. On the short side, again use your legs for bend and impulsion.
6. Repeat the long side with no leg aids.
7. At first you may proceed around the arena in a series of lurches. In the short term, *this does not matter.* As you keep doing this exercise, the horse will begin to keep going on the long sides without continual aids to support him, and your leg aids will be met with better reactions when you *do* use them.

## Common faults:

- *The rider finds it hard to lose the habit of 'scrubbing' with the legs.* Doing less is often harder than doing more – try pressing down more onto your stirrups, and even take your legs away from the horse's sides to gain more control over them.

Diagram labels:
C
H – X Start to use legs    Stop X – M using legs
E – I    I – B
K – X Stop using legs    Start to use legs X – F
A

- *The rider is reluctant to use a sharp enough aid when the horse slows down.* Remember, if you are sharp enough once, in future you will be able to use lighter, softer aids instead of needing to continually use your legs just to keep moving.

## TOP TIP

Whenever you find yourself working too hard, repeat this exercise to reinforce the lesson before returning to your routine.

# DIAGNOSTIC AND THERAPEUTIC EXERCISES

## 19. TURN AROUND THE FOREHAND

Walk.

### Aims:

- To check understanding of, or teach/confirm the correct response to a sideways displacing leg aid.
- To increase the depth of the sideways straddling motion of the inside hind leg when crossed **in front** of the outside hind leg.

### How to:

1. Unlike turn **on** the forehand (done at halt), this exercise is performed at walk. The front legs describe a small circle approximately 1–2m diameter, with the hind legs moving around a larger circle. The inside hind leg passes *in front* of the outside hind.

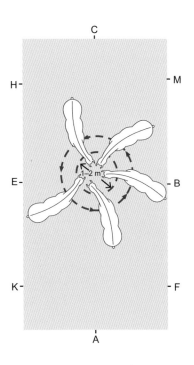

2. Open the inside rein to create a *slight* neck bend.
3. Keep the outside hand inwards and forwards to the crest to allow the bend whilst controlling the outside shoulder.
4. With the inside leg, ask the horse to move his hindquarters to the side. If the neck bend is to the left, the quarters will move towards the right.
5. Allow a little forward motion, to create the small circle with the forelegs.
6. If the horse struggles, initially allow the circle to be larger.
7. Request deliberate steps, not spinning around. Each leg aid should create one inside hind leg step. You should be able to halt at any time you choose.
8. The rider's outside leg should hang loosely, but not poke forward.

### Common faults:

- *Rider is too strong with the rein aids.* This causes tension and may stop the horse from obeying the leg aid. Relax the contact *before* applying the leg.
- *The horse moves too much forwards rather than sideways.* Exaggerate the open position of the inside rein and squeeze the outside rein (half-halt) in the same moment as you apply the inside leg.
- *The horse does not respond to the inside leg.* Take the reins in the outside hand and reach back and down with the schooling whip. Tap the hind leg at the same moment as you use the inside leg.
- *The horse steps backwards.* The rein contact may be too strong – walk a small circle and introduce the sideways motion while moving forwards.

### Combine with other exercises:

*See* exercise #34.

# 20. QUARTER LINES AND INSIDE TRACKS

Walk, trot, and canter.

## Aims:

- Working away from the psychological support of the track is an excellent way of determining the straightness of the horse, and the rider's control of both shoulders and haunches.

## How to:

### Inside track

1. Ride large around the arena.
2. Turn onto a line *one metre* inside the track.
3. Ride straight along this line without allowing the horse to drift back to the track. You may need to increase the weight in your inside stirrup, and/or be firmer with your outside rein against the shoulder, to prevent drift.

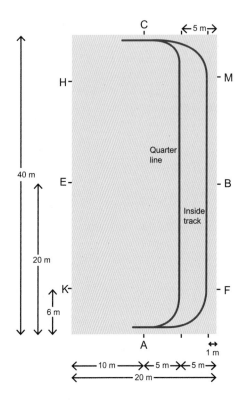

4. Repeat on several consecutive inner tracks until the horse starts to stay where you put him, and not try to fall to the track.

### Quarter line

1. From going large, turn onto the quarter, or three-quarter line. These are 5m from the track, so equidistant between the track and the centre line.
2. Ride straight, and check for drift in either direction. Try putting a marker on the fence at each end of these lines, so you have a visual point to aim at.

## Common faults:

- *Loss of straightness.* Ensure you ride positively forward without hurrying – the horse will travel straighter when going forward.
- *Horse falls towards one or other shoulder.* Keep his neck and shoulders straight by pressing the rein against the shoulder he tries to bulge onto.
- *In canter, the quarters swing in.* Put more weight into the inside stirrup and press the outside rein against his neck and shoulder to move his shoulders in front of his haunches. *Never* try to straighten by pushing the hindquarters out – this disengages the hind legs.

> ## TOP TIP
>
> Ride these lines between other exercises to check out the horse's straightness. The straighter the horse becomes, the more forward power he will develop as a result of using both hind legs evenly and equally.

# 21. 20m FIGURE OF EIGHT

Walk, trot and canter with a change of lead over X.

## Aims:

- A good diagnostic for comparing the horse's bend in the two directions.
- Checking that he can change bend without losing balance.

This versatile exercise can be ridden with, or without, transitions to:

- Add interest.
- Sharpen up the horse's responses.

## How to:

1. On the right rein, begin a 20m circle at A.
2. Just before X, straighten up so that you are facing directly towards B.

3. One stride after X, ride a 20m circle left.
4. When you return to X, again straighten for a couple of strides so you are riding straight towards B.
5. One stride after X, ride onto a 20m circle right.
6. You can complete the exercise when you arrive at A, or continue around the circle and keep repeating the pattern for as long as you wish.

## Common faults:

- *There is a loss of balance through the change of direction.* Ride the pattern in a slower gait and take plenty of time changing your aids: as you approach X change your diagonal, just before X use your new inside leg to ask for the new bend, at X put your weight into your new inside stirrup, in the stride after X turn your shoulders to the new direction.

- *The horse struggles with the changes of bend.* Start asking for the bend change with the new inside leg *before* X, so it is already in place before you make the change of direction.

- *The bend is not equal in the two directions.* Spend more time working on improving the bend on the stiffer side – you could ride two circles on the stiff side to every one on the more supple side.

## Combine with other exercises:

Add in trot-walk-trot transitions, placed with the walk steps over X. *See exercise #15 for how to perform transitions that include a change of direction.*

At a later stage of training, in canter, add in canter-trot-canter transitions in the same place, making a change of canter lead in addition to the direction change.

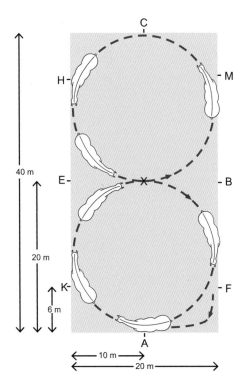

# 22. SQUARES

Walk, trot and canter.

## Aims:

- To address control of the horse's outside shoulder.
- To teach the value of riding corners: every corner offers a chance to gain engagement and balance.

## How to:

1. Ride a 20m square.
2. In the 20m × 40m arena on the right rein, 10m after E (halfway between E and the corner) make a 90-degree right turn and proceed straight across the arena.
3. Make a 90-degree right turn onto the track.
4. 10m after B, make a 90-degree right turn across the arena.
5. Make another 90-degree right turn onto the track.
6. Repeat.
7. In the 20m × 60m arena, turn right at E, right at B, right 8m after P (4m before F), and right again at the next track.
8. Make the turns only as tight as your horse can manage without losing balance or impulsion. As these qualities and his suppleness improve you will be able to make tighter turns.

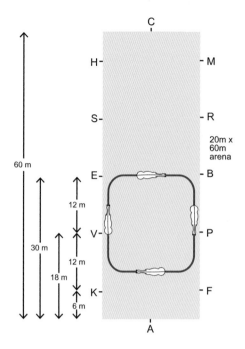

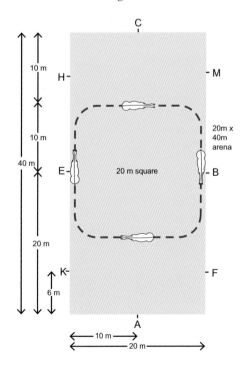

## Common faults:

- *The rider asks for too tight a turn, causing the horse to lose balance. See above,* and make your turns wider until your horse is more supple and balanced.
- *The horse falls out on the turns.* You need more control of the outside shoulder. Close your upper arm firmly to your side and turn your shoulders to the inside to press your outside rein against the horse's neck. Make sure your weight is in your inside seat bone and stirrup.
- *The horse falls in during the turns.* Use more inside leg to ride forward around the turns, initially making them bigger to help maintain balance.
- *The horse overturns, ending up on the wrong line.* As you turn, look at the next point you are going to, and ride forward out of the turn sooner.

## TOP TIP

As the horse's suppleness, balance and engagement improve, you can reduce the size of the square to make him really attentive to your turning aids. Eventually you may be able to ride a 10m square, but never go smaller than the horse can manage with relative ease.

# 23. 10m CIRCLES

**Walk, trot and canter.**

## Aims:

All horses should be able to perform these in walk. For horses progressing their training beyond the most basic, in trot and canter 10m circles become a simple but effective tool to address several increases in physical demand:

- Suppleness.
- Connection from leg to hand to secure the outline.
- Engagement and power.
- Strength.
- Collection.

## How to:

1. *See* the instructions for riding a 20m circle, exercise #1.

2. To ride a 10m circle instead of a 20m, simply increase the degree of turn in your upper body.

3. A 10m circle begun anywhere from the track will touch the centre line. A 10m circle at A or C will touch both quarter lines.

## Common faults:

- *As for the 20m circle (#1).*

- *The horse struggles with the degree of bend by stiffening, resisting, or is incapable of bending to this degree.* Ride slightly larger circles at first, such as 12m, until he finds that easier, before reducing to 10m.

- *He swings his hindquarters out, or crosses the inside hind leg over in front of the outside hind.* Be more conscientious about your outside leg position (*see* exercise #1), and press it against his ribcage to create body bend behind you.

- *He loses impulsion.* This may happen at first, because the pattern brings the hind leg further forward under the body – do not punish him or be unfair in your demands. As he becomes stronger, he will find it easier. Once he *is* stronger, be insistent that he maintains the tempo and energy of the gait throughout the circle.

## Combine with other exercises:

Because the 10m circle increases engagement and creates a more secure connection, it is the ideal exercise to set up many others, such as transitions, medium trot and canter, and lateral work.

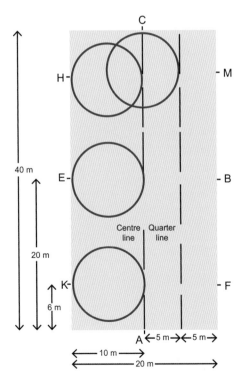

# 24. SMALL CIRCLES IN EVERY CORNER

Walk, trot and canter.

## Aims:

- To teach both horse and rider to travel around every corner with an inside bend.

## How to:

1. Ride large around the arena.
2. In each corner, ride a small circle. The size is not critical (between 10m and 12m is ideal) – pick whatever size the horse can achieve without losing rhythm.
3. Stay on the circle until the inside bend is established.
4. Move onto the next corner and repeat.
5. The value is in the repetition – the horse will start to anticipate the circle as he enters each corner, and pick up the inside bend more quickly.
6. Keep riding the circles in each corner until you feel the bend is easy, and then remove the occasional circle.
7. At the end of this exercise, you should be able to ride around the arena with inside bend in every corner, without needing to perform any circles.

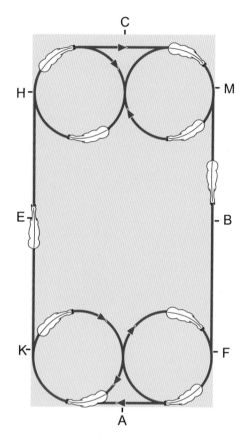

## Common faults:

- *The horse struggles with the small circles.* Ride the exercise in a slower gait – even a very stiff horse can manage circles of this size in walk.
- *The horse does not go into the corner.* Place markers just to the inside of the corners as a guide to ride around.
- *Once you cease riding the circles, the horse no longer bends in every corner.* As soon as you feel that the inside bend could be better, simply put in a small circle (or two) before leaving a corner.

## Combine with other exercises:

Use the small circle in the second corner of the short side to build up extra energy and ride out of it into medium trot down the long side. At the end of the medium, use the small circle in the first corner to help re-collect the horse.

Alternatively, use the small circle in the corner to create the bend for shoulder-in down the long side.

> ## TOP TIP
>
> Return to this exercise every so often, to remind both the horse and yourself that corners should be ridden accurately with inside bend, and not just coasted around without care or attention.

# 25. ALTERNATING 10m CIRCLES ON THE CENTRE LINE

Walk and trot.

## Aims:

Only attempt this exercise once the horse can perform 10m circles with relative ease, and try it first time in walk.

- To review the equality of the horse's bending in both directions.
- To challenge steering: re-finding a straight centre line coming out of a small circle is not as easy as it looks!
- In trot this is also a strengthening and stamina-building exercise.

## How to:

In the 20m × 40m arena:

1. From the left rein, turn up the centre line at A and straighten the horse.
2. With a small half-halt (vibration) on the left rein, prepare a left bend.
3. Before X, ride a 10m circle left.
4. Continue straight up the centre line.
5. After X, use a small half-halt on the right rein to prepare the new bend.
6. Between X and C, ride a 10m circle right.
7. Continue up the centre line and turn right at C.

In the 20m × 60m arena you should be able to ride four circles in alternating directions on a single centre line.

## Common faults:

- *The horse falls in on one circle, and out on the other.* See exercise #1 for corrections.
- *You struggle with straightening onto the centre line as you leave the circle.* In the 10m circles, your weight should be towards the inside. As you leave each circle remember to sit centrally and ride positively forward – see exercise #11.
- *The horse's hindquarters swing out on the circles.* Move your outside leg back to control the hindquarters.
- *The horse stiffens, and/or hollows.* Review riding slightly larger circles to improve his suppleness before attempting again.

## Combine with other exercises:

Use this exercise as a more challenging way of changing rein. Performed well, the circles will give you increased engagement, so you will arrive on the new rein with extra power for your next exercise, such as an upward transition, or a medium trot.

At a more advanced level, in canter, combine with either simple, or flying changes between the circles.

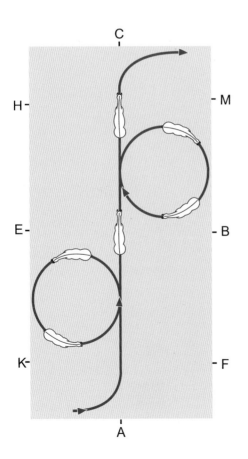

# 26. SATELLITE CIRCLES

**Walk and trot.**

## Aims:

- Asking for frequent changes of bend is highly suppling.
- The unusual pattern adds interest to a work session.
- You can use either two, or four, satellite circles depending on the flexibility, and the level of concentration, of the horse.

## How to:

1. On the right rein, ride a 20m circle in the centre of the arena, at E.
2. For two satellite circles – as you cross the centre line, turn away onto a left rein 10m circle.
3. As you re-join the centre line, return to the right rein 20m circle.

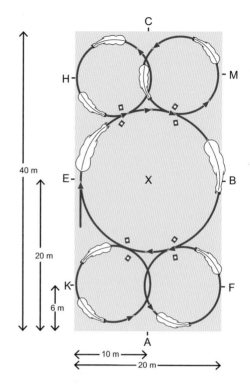

4. Next time you cross the centre line, repeat the 10m satellite circle.
5. For four satellites, you need to turn away onto 10m circles at a point on the 20m circle that is halfway between E and the centre line, halfway between the centre line and B, and so on (*see* diagram).

## Common faults:

- *The horse struggles or resists the changes of bend.* Ride only the two-satellite version at first. Start asking for the change of flexion earlier so the horse is more prepared when you ask for the change of direction. Review the procedure in exercise #6.
- *You find it difficult to ride the shape accurately.* Put out markers as suggested on the diagram to give you visual aids to ride around.

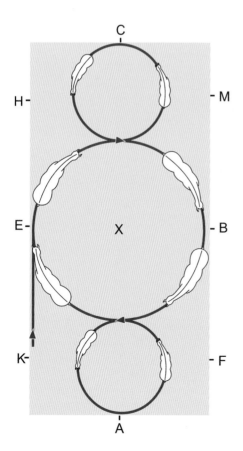

## TOP TIP

Pop in one of these satellite circles any time you feel the need for increased suppleness or more equal acceptance of the bit on both sides of the mouth.

# 27. CONTINENTAL SERPENTINES

**Walk and trot.**

## Aims:

- To increase suppleness, rhythm and balance, by performing the frequent changes of bend demanded by a serpentine with direct changes from one bend to the other, instead of with a straight line joining each loop.

## How to:

1. Start a serpentine.
2. Instead of straightening across the centre line, continue a little further around the loop before changing to the other bend and beginning a loop in the new direction. *See* diagram.

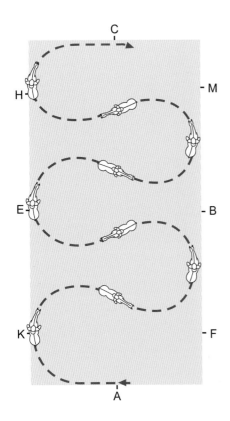

3. Prepare the direction change with a small half-halt, and then try to achieve the bend and direction change in one stride.
4. At first, just ride a few loops to get the idea of the pattern.
5. Once you are both comfortable with the shape, and because you are looping back on yourself, you can fit in as many loops as you wish.

## Common faults:

- *Loss of balance or resistance in the bend change.* Review exercise #12, and take a step or two longer for the bend change. Reduce to one stride when you can achieve the change with balance and harmony.
- *The horse speeds up as you change direction.* Do not rush the change in your aiding or you may startle the horse. Also ensure the horse remains upright, not leaning to one side or the other.

## Combine with other exercises:

Try putting small circles into the peaks of each loop as a suppling exercise.

At more advanced levels, ride this in canter with flying changes between the loops.

# 28. CHANGE CANTER LEAD ON THE DIAGONAL WITH GUIDE POLES

## Aims:

- To assist with the horse's straightness in canter transitions performed on straight lines.
- To check that the horse is picking up the correct canter lead from the rider's aids, and not simply from the direction of travel.

## How to:

1. Have poles positioned as in the diagram.
2. Pick up right lead canter on the FAK short side, and then ride down the long side.
3. Turn onto the MXK diagonal.
4. Before X, transition to trot.
5. Over X, establish balance and rhythm in trot.
6. After X, pick up left-lead canter.
7. Canter around the KAF short side, and either travel down the long side (if the canter energy needs to be more established), and repeat the pattern on the HXF diagonal.
8. Or turn immediately onto the FXH diagonal and repeat the change of lead over X.

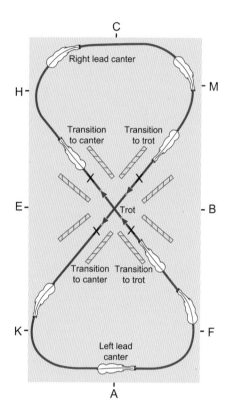

## Common faults:

- *The horse picks up the wrong canter lead.* Make sure your aiding is very clear, and your weight is in your new inside stirrup. If the problem persists, return to making transitions on large circles with very clear aiding before trying again.
- *The horse runs into canter.* Be very sure to balance the trot before asking for the strike off – if the horse is already running in trot, the problem will only get bigger in the transition. Keep a slightly firmer contact as you ask for canter.

## TOP TIP

Once the horse is performing the exercise with relative ease, remove some of the ground poles. Keep just the ones on the side towards which the horse is prone to drifting – that is, if he tends to lean on his left shoulder, keep the poles that will be on his left-hand side while doing this pattern. Eventually, remove them all and continue to ride the exercise.

# 29. REIN BACK BETWEEN POLES

### Aims:

- A good diagnostic for the horse's straightness.
- Developing equal strength in both hind legs.
- Teaches lowering of the croup.
- Ridden between poles, corrects any tendency to swing sideways.

### How to:

1. Place two poles side by side, off the track, and 1m apart. Raised poles are ideal so that he cannot step on them.
2. Ride between the poles and halt just before the hindquarters exit the poles.

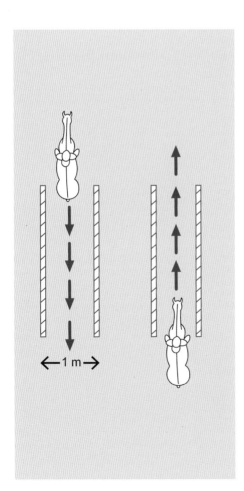

3. Make sure the horse is soft and round in the halt. If not, lower his neck before continuing.
4. Slightly lighten your seat and draw both your legs slightly back.
5. Close your fingers on the reins but **do not** pull, or hold a tight or rigid contact.
6. Tap the horse with both legs while maintaining closed fingers.
7. Rein back until his shoulders reach the end of the poles.
8. Sit back into the saddle, move your legs forward, and relax your hands to ride forward again.

### Common faults:

- *The horse resists the contact.* Play the reins softly, vibrating them in turn – **never pull back.** Make sure his neck lowers before asking him to go back again – a hollow back is uncomfortable, which will discourage the horse from performing rein back in the future.
- *He refuses to step back.* If the horse is not clear what is being asked, use an assistant on the ground to put a hand against his chest to encourage him to step back.
- *His hindquarters swing to the side.* If his quarters swing left, take your left leg further back than your right. Alternatively, with both legs parallel, use the left leg more strongly. In extreme cases, take the left leg further back *and* use it more strongly.
- *He goes wide behind as he steps back.* Move the poles closer together, until he cannot widen behind without touching a pole.

### Combine with other exercises:

Rein back is an excellent method of setting up engaged upward transitions, so vary the gait in which you come out of the exercise.

# ENGAGE THE HORSE'S CORE MUSCLES

## 30. VOLTE (SMALL CIRCLE)

Walk.

### Aims:

- Core engagement is essential for the health of the horse's physical structure: skeleton, joints, muscles, tendons and ligaments.
- A genuine outline is impossible without engagement of the horse's core muscles. The back cannot be raised, and so the spine will sag downwards, putting the horse at risk of spinal problems, and the pelvis will be at an open angle with the hind legs out behind the body where they cannot give support.
- It *is* possible to put a horse into an outline that *looks* superficially correct by creating an arch in the horse's neck, usually by the use of gadgets or strong hands, but unless there is support from the core muscles, there can be no true biomechanical functionality.

### How to:

1. In walk, ride a small circle – six metres is ideal, as this aligns the spine in such a fashion that the inside hind leg will step into an engaged position beneath the body.
2. Open the inside rein, and bend the neck, slightly more than normal.
3. Press the outside hand forward enough to allow the bend, but keep it close to the shoulder for control.
4. Keep the steps slow and deliberate. The goal is that the horse carries weight on each hind leg in turn.
5. When the horse chews the bit and offers to lower the neck, allow him to take the reins down into a stretch.
6. Ride out of the circle with the horse in the stretched position.
7. Change rein, and then re-gather the reins and repeat in the new direction.

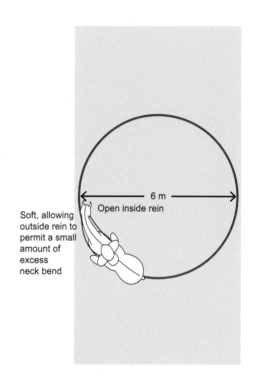

6 m

Open inside rein

Soft, allowing outside rein to permit a small amount of excess neck bend

### Common faults:

- *The horse does not take the neck down.* Check you are keeping all the components in place – no speed, a good degree of bend with an open inside rein, and no drifting out of the circle. Then just stay there. Sometimes it takes a while for this exercise to work, but if you do it correctly, the effects are unavoidable.

### TOP TIP

Use this in your warm-up to get the horse's core muscles woken up before you progress to trot.

# 31. VOLTE WITH SHOULDER-IN (OR HAUNCHES-IN)

Walk.

## Aims:

- As explained in the previous exercise (#30), core engagement is essential to the health of the horse's body.
- This is a variation on exercise #30 for the more educated horse, which can give you a quicker result.
- It is also appropriate and effective as a remedial exercise for a horse that has already learned more advanced movements, but *without* correct core engagement.

## How to:

1. In walk, ride a 10m circle.
2. Develop shoulder-in on the circle. Take care this is achieved correctly, by bringing the shoulders inwards, onto a smaller arc, and not by swinging the hindquarters out.
3. Stay in this position at a slow, deliberate walk. Make the horse wait with his body weight carried fully on his inside hind before allowing the next step.
4. Once he starts to chew the bit and lower his neck, permit him to take the reins and stretch down.
5. When he is stable in the stretch, walk out of the circle and change the rein.
6. Repeat in the opposite direction.

## Common faults:

- *The horse swings his hindquarters out.* Keep a clear outside leg position, so that when his rear end moves outward, your outside leg is ready to catch them and prevent him from escaping behind.
- *The horse tries to hurry off the inside hind.* Keep him at a slower speed – each step should be deliberate and controlled.

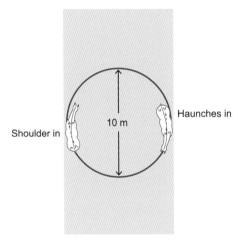

Shoulder in | 10 m | Haunches in

### TOP TIP

With some horses, this exercise is more effective when ridden in-haunches in around the 10m circle, rather than shoulder-in.

# 32. RIDING IN A STRETCHED OUTLINE

Walk, trot and canter.

## Aims:

- For the horse already educated in using his core muscles, riding in a low, stretched position will be sufficient to engage his core during warm-up.

Correct stretching involves:
- Putting the poll and neck *below* the withers.
- Keeping enough contact that the horse is *slightly* flexed at the poll, and not poking his nose forward.
- Keeping his nose *slightly* in front of the vertical, with no over-curling or drawing back.

## How to:

1. Invite the horse to stretch. If this is his usual routine, he will offer it in walk as soon as you move away from the mounting block.
2. If not, invite him by riding a circle and, with low positioned hands, move the bit softly in the corners of his mouth to ask him to chew the bit.
3. Once he starts to chew, his poll will flex. Allow the reins longer to permit him to lower his head.
4. Once in stretch, ride suppling patterns – curves, circles, turns, serpentines – as well as going larger around the track.
5. He should stretch in walk, trot and canter, until his muscles and joints are fully warmed up, before you gather him together ready for work.

## Common faults:

- *The horse is reluctant to stretch down.* Review exercises #30 and/or #31.
- *He pokes his nose forward.* Keep a little more contact, and gently move the bit in the corners of his mouth to encourage him to chew the bit – flexion at the poll is only possible when the jaw muscles relax.
- *He over-curls and draws his neck back.* Reduce speed – over-curling can be a symptom of lack of

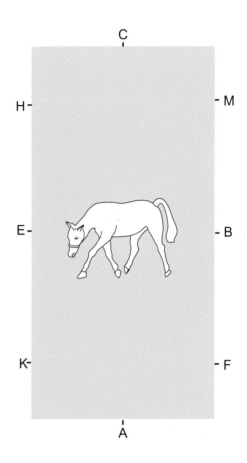

balance. Try to keep a contact with his mouth, but also a feeling of pushing forward, to push his nose away from you.

## Combine with other exercises:

Stretching should always be the first portion of any warm-up, to enable muscles and joints to come up to working temperature without stress, and so avoid exercise-induced injuries. It should also be employed in the warm-down at the end of every session to promote muscle health.

# LEG YIELD PATTERNS

## 33. PATTERNS TO TEACH LEG YIELD

**Walk and trot.**

### Aims:

Leg yielding is a versatile exercise that can be used to:
- Teach a horse to move sideways away from the leg.
- Teach a rider how to move a horse sideways.
- Increase engagement of the inside hind leg.
- Improve suppleness of the lower back and hind limbs when ridden with a bend rather than a straight body.

### How to:

1. Ride along the inside track.
2. Turn your shoulders slightly towards the inside of the arena.
3. *Stop* using the outside leg but continue using the inside leg at the girth, in the same speed and intensity as before, to push the horse towards the track.
4. Keep your weight in the *inside* seat bone to encourage him to step under your weight.
5. On the horse's stiff rein, allow the outside rein a little forward to encourage him outward.
6. On the horse's flexible side, keep the outside rein firmly against the neck and shoulder to discourage him from falling onto his outside shoulder.
7. Advance this by starting gradually further away from the track – first, a few metres, then from the quarter line, and eventually from the centre line.

### Common faults:

- *The horse does not move sideways.* Check that your outside leg is passive or this will discourage him from moving over. If he still does not respond, go back a stage and ride a turn around the forehand (#19) to re-confirm that he must move away from your leg, before returning to this exercise.
- *The horse rushes.* You probably speeded up your leg aid, or pushed too hard. Use your inside leg aid

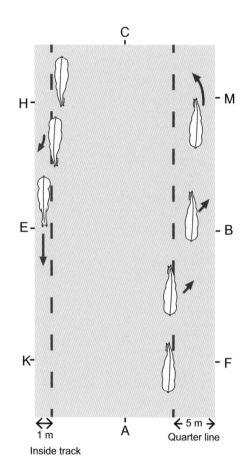

at the same speed and strength as before the leg yield.
- *The horse runs out through his outside shoulder.* Keep your outside rein firm, with your outside hand against his withers, and your outside *elbow* closed against your torso. Open your inside rein. Intersperse a few steps of leg yield with a few strides ridden straight forward.

### Combine with other exercises:

Leg yielding is a good preparation for a trot to canter transition, or a medium trot.

# 34. TURN AROUND THE FOREHAND INTO LEG YIELD

**Walk only.**

## Aims:

- By connecting the turn around the forehand (exercise #19), where the horse moves his hindquarters away from the driving leg, into a leg yield, this combined pattern helps the horse to understand that he must cross his legs in leg yield.

## How to:

1. On the right rein, turn onto the centre line at C.
2. At G, ride a **full** turn around the forehand (#19), moving the horse away from your right leg, so that his hindquarters travel towards the left (turn around the forehand left).
3. Once you have completed the full turn, ride *immediately* into a leg yield to the left, aiming to arrive at the track by B (long arena), or between B and F (short arena).

## Common faults:

- *The turn around the forehand is very large.* Do not worry too much about the size, provided the horse crosses his hind legs in response to your inside leg aid.
- *The horse falls onto his outside shoulder during the leg yield.* Keep your outside rein firmly pressed against his neck and shoulder.
- *There is no leg crossing in the leg yield.* Repeat the turn around the forehand after just a few steps of incorrect leg yield, provided that you are far enough away from the wall to accommodate the length of the horse's body, and go back into leg yield again.

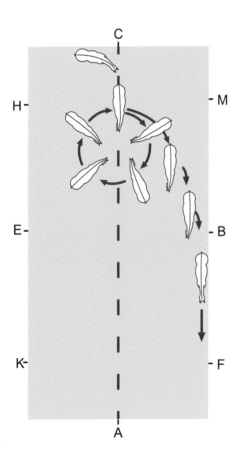

## TOP TIP

Once the horse understands to cross the legs within the leg yield, you can dispense with the preparatory turn around the forehand. Conversely, if he returns to performing leg yield *without* crossing his legs, repeat this pattern as often as needed.

# 35. 'BABY' LEG YIELD INTO CIRCLE

Walk, trot and canter.

## Aim:

- To create more suppleness on the horse's stiff side.
- This is a therapeutic exercise. You will be using the horse's natural inclination to fall towards the track to achieve increased bend. **Do not** worry about containing the outside shoulder.

## How to:

1. Ride this exercise **only on your horse's stiffer rein**.
2. Using his natural inclination to fall towards the track, ride a diagonal line from C to E (left rein), or C to B (right rein).
3. On this line, *allow/encourage* the outside shoulder to fall outward. The short/tight side of the horse's body will lengthen, and the long/weak muscles on the inside will contract, creating body bend.
4. Use your inside leg to push him outwards along this line, further encouraging the above use of his muscles.
5. Upon arrival at the track, turn immediately onto a large circle (15m–20m) and continue to push his ribcage out, using your inside leg exactly as if you were still leg yielding outwards.
6. Complete the circle and then go large to A and repeat.
7. *Or* ride a half-20m circle, then go large to return to C and repeat.

## Common faults:

- *Not achieving the correct line.* Getting the turn at A or C correct is critical to positioning the horse's body for this exercise to be effective. As you turn, point his shoulders towards the letter you are aiming for.
- *Not allowing the shoulder to lead enough (especially in canter).* It is essential that you let the outside shoulder lead excessively to achieve the desired effect.
- *Trying to make him parallel with the long side.* Don't. You must allow him to fall onto his outside shoulder for this exercise to work.

## Combine with other exercises:

Ride this pattern in trot to set up a canter transition – especially useful for helping a young horse strike-off into a correctly bent and balanced canter.

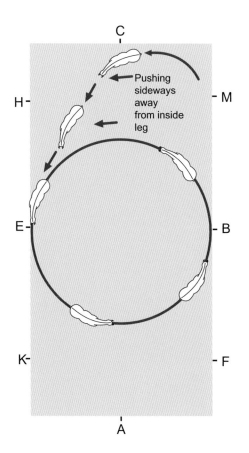

Pushing sideways away from inside leg

## TOP TIP

When you make your initial turn at either A or C, start pushing sideways *before* you complete the turn – do not straighten up first.

# 36. LEG YIELD ALONG THE WALL

**Walk and trot.**

## Aims:

- To supple the horse's lower back and hind legs.
- To teach a correct response to the sideways displacing leg aid on a horse that is prone to running forward as either an evasion or a misunderstanding.

## How to:

1. On the left rein, along the long side FBM.
2. As you travel through the corner preceding F, create a small *right* flexion in the horse's poll.
3. Do not fully straighten onto the long side: the aim is to travel along the track at an angle of around 30 degrees to the fence.
4. Maintain a small open-rein position with the inside (right) rein (remember: *inside* refers to the horse's bend, and not to the direction of travel around the arena) to maintain right flexion.
5. The outside (left) rein should be inwards and *slightly* forwards towards the crest, to keep the neck *almost* straight and control the outside shoulder.
6. Apply the inside (right) leg at the girth to displace the horse sideways.
7. The outside (left) leg should hang passively but not poke forwards.

## Common faults:

- *The horse falls onto his outside shoulder, offering excessive neck bend.* Keep a firmer outside rein to keep the neck straighter, but not so strong that you stop the horse from moving forward.
- *The quarters swing too much sideways, so the horse ends up facing the wall and stops.* Soften both rein contacts to allow the shoulders to keep moving in advance of the hindquarters. You may also need to use a softer leg aid.
- *The horse fights the contact or panics.* Use a softer rein aid, and allow the fence to do the job of controlling the horse's desire to evade by running forwards.

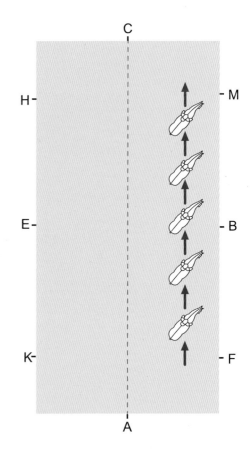

- *You struggle to get any angle.* Persist with your positioning aids. Some horses, especially physically stiff ones, will take time to develop sufficient suppleness to achieve the angle.

## TOP TIP

If the horse struggles, use less strength in the aiding, and not more. For the exercise to be beneficial, there must be a relaxed cooperation.

# 37. LEG YIELD, APPROACHED FROM THE OPPOSITE DIRECTION

Walk and trot.

## Aims:

- This pattern is how leg yield is presented in most competition tests.
- A good method to help prevent the horse from throwing his weight onto the outside shoulder at the start of a leg yield.

## How to:

1. From the right rein, turn onto the centre line at C.
2. In rising trot, change your diagonal.
3. Move the horse's shoulders towards the direction of travel (right) by taking both hands *slightly* towards the right, which will also create a small left flexion.

4. Bring your hands back into position left to control the shoulder as you apply your left leg at the girth, keeping your weight in your left seat bone and stirrup. Stop using your right leg.
5. The horse should now be moving towards the right, with a small flexion to the left at the poll, in leg yield right.

You can also start this pattern from a half-circle onto the centre line at any position from the long side.

## Common faults:

- *The horse falls onto the outside shoulder.* You may have moved the shoulders too far into the lead before you started the leg yield. Keep your outside rein more firmly against the neck and shoulder, to control the outside shoulder and keep the neck straight.
- *The horse starts the leg yield with the quarters leading.* You either did not move the shoulders into the lead far enough, or at all. Make sure to position them slightly into the lead *before* asking for sideways movement.
- *The horse loses balance at the start.* Take more time to straighten, and then position his shoulders, before starting the leg yield.
- *He arrives at the track too early.* Use a less strong inside leg. If necessary, you might also need a *little* outside leg to keep him moving forward as well as sideways.

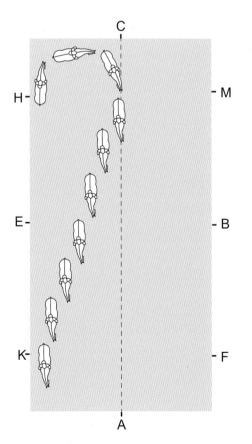

### TOP TIP

If the horse does not move enough sideways, you may well have the quarters in the lead – the horse cannot travel sideways with the quarters leading, only with the shoulders leading.

# 38. LEG YIELD ZIGZAGS

**Walk and trot.**

## Aims:

- Promotes stretching and relaxation in a stiff and/ or tense horse.
- To loosen the horse's frame.
- Good for re-confirming and improving the horse's response to the sideways displacing leg aid.

## How to:

This can be performed in a variety of places in the arena, and with different numbers of leg yields, depending on the suppleness and response of the horse, and the length of the arena.

### *Two-leg zigzag:*

1. From F, ride leg yield left (right flexion) away from the track.

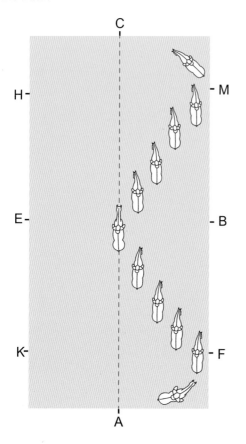

2. At the quarter or centre line, depending on how much sideways travel you have achieved, straighten the horse and change the flexion to the left.
3. Move the shoulders to the right until they are fractionally in the lead before leg yielding right to M.

### *Three-leg zigzag:*

1. Turn on the centre line at A and leg yield to the left (right flexion).
2. At the quarter line, change flexion and move the shoulders to the right.
3. Leg yield right, to the opposite quarter line.
4. Change flexion and shoulder position again, and leg yield left, returning to the centre line at G.
5. At C turn right, because you will already have a right flexion.

You can do these anywhere in the arena, riding as many metres to the side as you choose before changing direction. The more changes of direction you perform, the greater the suppling effect on the horse.

## Common faults:

- *Not waiting until the horse is established in leg yield – rhythm, position, flexion and balance – before changing direction.* Always wait until the leg yield feels easy before changing direction.
- *The horse struggles to change to one direction.* By nature, horses lean on one shoulder, which makes the changeover more difficult one way than the other. Go back to single leg yields and practise straightening at the end.

## TOP TIP

If you struggle to get the horse to leave the wall when attempting to leg yield inwards away from the track, try starting from the inside track instead to reduce the psychological draw of the track.

# 39. CANTER PLIÉ (CANTER LEG YIELD)

## Aims:

Use the horse's natural desire to fall towards the outside shoulder to:

- Induce bend in the body, to improve lateral suppleness on the horse's stiff side. *If this is the purpose, then only ride this exercise on the stiffer rein.*
- To loosen and/or reduce tension in the horse's lower back.

- To adjust the landing of a hind hoof that habitually lands on the ground excessively heel first (*see #46*).

## How to:

**Note:** That to travel sideways in canter, the horse's shoulders *must* be positioned in advance of the haunches. Due to the sequence of legs at canter, the horse cannot cross his legs, but must jump sideways like a knife dicing a tomato.

1. In right-lead canter, turn at C.
2. Aim for just after B (long arena) or F (short arena).
3. With a small inside flexion, yield *both* reins by pushing your hands forwards.
4. Allow the horse to 'fall' towards his outside shoulder.
5. Keep your weight on your inside seat bone, and use your inside leg at the girth to encourage him to move sideways.

## Common faults:

- *Loss of balance.* Do not worry too much about this at this stage – this is a remedial exercise, and not a finished product. Much of its value is in using the horse's body weight to give him an experience of moving with contraction of his inside ribcage muscles, that is with body bend.
- *The horse breaks out of canter.* Recover canter and repeat, using seat and leg to sustain canter. Falling out of the pace can be a form of evasion, as well as a consequence of balance loss.
- *The canter becomes rushed.* At the end of each plié, ride a 20m or 15m circle to regain control before repeating.

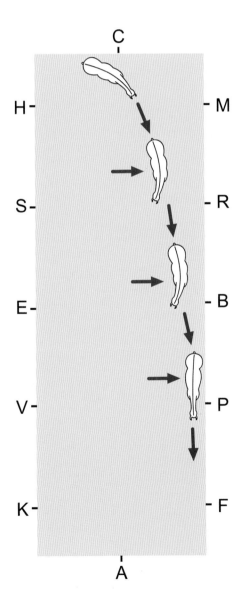

**TOP TIP**

In a horse with a more advanced degree of balance this exercise can be used to create a degree of collection. Keep the outside shoulder a little more under control, sit very tall and use the inside leg to bring the inside hind under the body.

# COUNTER-CANTER PATTERNS

## 40. SHALLOW LOOPS IN CANTER

### Aims:

- The first introductory exercise to counter-canter.
- Increase engagement. To maintain canter with the leading hind leg on the outside of the curve, that leg must take a longer step than when it is on the inside of a curve.

### How to:

1. **Remember**: in counter-canter, *inside* relates to the side the horse is flexed towards, and not to the direction of travel around the arena.
2. Review the shape of the figure in exercise #8.
3. Ride the same line, starting with a very shallow loop (1–2m) before gradually progressing to increasingly deeper loops.
4. Unlike trot, **do not** change bend. Keep the head and neck positioned towards the leading leg, with the horse's nose directly in front of his inside knee.
5. As you approach the change of direction, keep your body position constant and your weight clearly in your *inside* seat bone.
6. Maintaining your upper body position, take both hands towards the outside of the arena to move the shoulders towards the new direction.
7. Once the direction change is achieved, replace your hands into their normal position.

### Common faults:

- *The horse breaks out of canter.* Use stronger seat and leg aids, but **do not** try to hold the horse together with the reins: this will block the hind leg from travelling fully forward.
- *The rider and/or horse lean towards the outside.* This will cause loss of balance, and possibly loss of canter. Focus on remaining upright relative to the ground, and not to the horse.

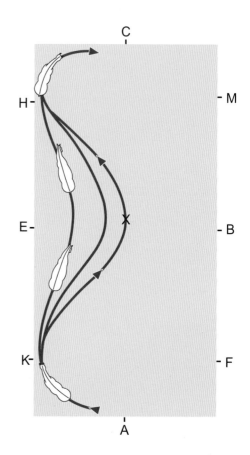

- *The rider uses too strong an inside rein in an attempt to 'push' the horse through the turn.* This blocks the leading hind leg and pushes the horse onto his outside shoulder, encouraging him to fall back towards the wall out of balance.
- *The rider changes the bend.* The horse will no longer be in counter-canter, merely incorrect canter lead.

### Combine with other exercises:

Once the loop is achieved, ride a 20m or a 15m circle at A or C. This aids relaxation and confirms the engagement resulting from the loop.

# 41. HALF-CIRCLE AND RETURN TO COUNTER-CANTER

## Aims:

- To develop the horse's balance.
- Strengthen the back muscles.
- Instil obedience to the aids.

## How to:

1. In left canter, towards the end of the long side near, or at, M, ride a half-circle of between 15m and 10m. Make the circle as small as the horse can manage without losing balance or impulsion.

2. From the end of the half-circle, ride a straight line back towards the track. In the long arena, aim as near to B as you can. In the short arena, aim to arrive between B and F.

3. Keep your weight towards the leading (left) leg.

4. Keep the horse positioned towards the leading leg, with just a mild neck bend.

5. Keep your right leg drawn back in an outside leg position.

6. Maintain the canter for as many strides as you are able to before returning to trot. At first, this might be two or three strides. Build up until you can keep it all the way to F.

7. Later on, as the horse's balance and strength develop, you can maintain the counter-canter through the first corner, and then eventually, through the entire short side.

## Common faults:

- *You lose the canter altogether.* Check that you maintained the aids as detailed above. On your next attempt, ride with a more positive seat aid – counter-canter is largely maintained by the seat.

- *The canter becomes disunited.* Your weight may have moved to the outside of the saddle, or your outside leg slipped forward. It may also be that the canter was insufficiently balanced before you attempted the pattern.

- *The horse performs a flying change.* Repeat calmly, with a slight exaggeration of your aiding, in particular weight and outside leg position.

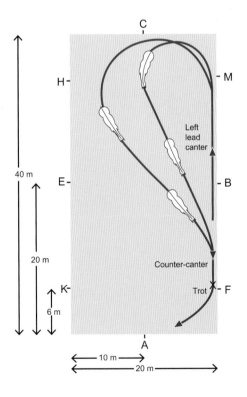

**TOP TIP**

If your horse offers a flying change, do not reprimand him! You may wish to teach him flying changes at a later date, so you should not discourage him at this stage.

# 42. CANTER FROM TRACK TO CENTRE LINE

## Aims:

A shallow counter-canter pattern, particularly useful for horses that:

- Lose balance.
- Become anxious.
- Fall out of canter.
- Disunite when faced with a return to the track.

## How to:

1. In the 60m arena, take left-lead canter.
2. Turn on a diagonal line from F towards X.
3. At X, join the centre line.
4. Keep your weight position in the saddle towards the side of the leading leg, and maintain the horse's bend during the turn onto the centre line. Simply move both hands *slightly* towards the right to turn the shoulders, before replacing them into their normal position.
5. Canter down the centre line and at C, turn left.
6. Either canter down the long side and repeat from F, or if the horse is balanced and calm, repeat immediately by turning at H and going to X.
7. An alternative line would be, for example, to turn at P and go to I.

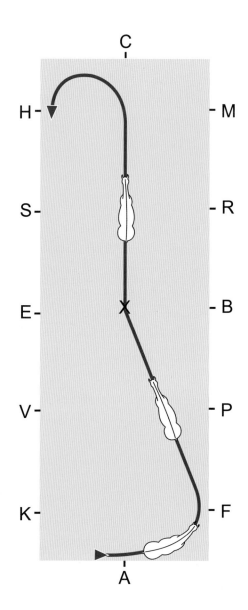

## Common faults:

- *As you attempt to turn onto the centre line, the horse loses balance, resulting in a wobbly centre line.* Be really conscientious about keeping your weight in the saddle towards the side of the leading canter leg, and bring your outside rein against the neck and shoulder immediately once the horse has begun the turn.
- *The canter loses jump.* Use your seat to maintain the canter speed, and quick leg aids to ask for more activity.
- *The horse struggles with the small turn at the end of the centre line.* Support him with a stronger inside leg to maintain impulsion, and make sure your outside leg is drawn back to keep control of his haunches and prevent them from swinging out.

## Combine with other exercises:

Following the turn at C, go forward to medium canter down the long side to regain a livelier canter, before repeating the exercise from the same end of the arena as before.

# 43. COUNTER-CANTER WITH SATELLITE CIRCLES

## Aims:

- A good exercise for horses not yet well-balanced in counter-canter, as they only have to travel half a circle in counter-canter before returning to true canter on the smaller circle, which then re-balances the horse before returning to counter-canter.

## How to:

1. In the 40m arena start to ride a 10m circle in right-lead canter at A.

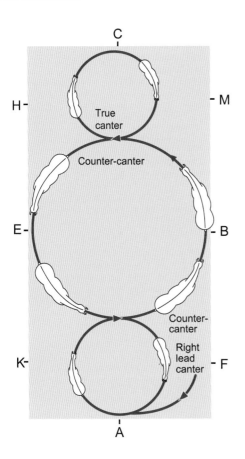

2. As you cross the centre line in the middle of the arena, turn away onto a 20m half-circle in counter-canter. This will touch the track at B.

3. *Do not* change the horse's bend, or your weight position in the saddle.

4. As you cross the next centre line, turn onto a 10m circle right at C in true canter.

5. When you return to the centre line, pick up a half-20m circle in counter-canter to touch the track at E.

6. Repeat.

## Common faults:

- *There is a loss of balance or stiffening in the counter-canter.* Make sure you have kept your weight position in the saddle towards the side of the leading leg, and not taken too strong a contact in your efforts to turn his shoulders, as this will block the hind legs.

- *The horse changes lead.* Check both of the above, and also ensure you do not have too much neck bend – this pushes the horse onto the outside shoulder, which invites the change.

## TOP TIP

If the horse does an unrequested flying change, *do not punish him*. There will come a time when you want the changes, so rather than discourage him, return to a simpler pattern, such as a shallow loop, to instil more obedience to your aids.

# MORE ADVANCED THERAPEUTIC LATERAL WORK TO ADJUST FOOTFALLS

## 44. SHOULDER-IN, TO TURN AROUND THE FOREHAND, TO SHOULDER-IN

Walk and trot.

### Aims:

- To loosen the horse's lower back.
- To increase the straddling of the hind legs.
- Far more difficult when ridden in trot, but will offer the biggest benefit.

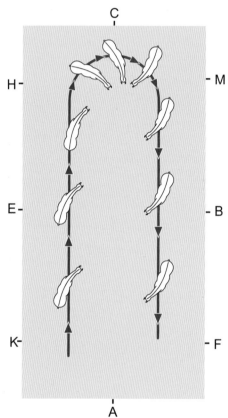

### How to:

1. In trot, ride shoulder-in up the three-quarter line.
2. About 10m before the end of the arena, perform a half-turn around the forehand. In trot, this may involve pressing your weight towards the rear of your seat to encourage the horse to lower his croup, with a firm outside rein to control the outside shoulder, along with an active inside leg aid to keep him in trot while he crosses the hind legs.
3. Once you complete a half-turn, head back towards the other end of the arena, again in shoulder-in. You may now be on the quarter line, or anywhere between the centre line and the track – this is unimportant when first riding this pattern.
4. Repeat the turnaround as you approach the end of the arena and go back into shoulder-in.
5. Keep repeating.
6. As the turnaround becomes easier, reduce its size, until you can ride up and down the arena a couple of metres either side of the centre line.

### Common faults:

- *The horse runs out through the shoulder during the turnaround.* The horse is evading the effect on the hind leg. Control the shoulder with a firm outside rein – as the horse's suppleness and ability to cross his hind legs improves, he will find the exercise easier.
- *You lose the trot.* Back up your leg aids with small, quick taps with the schooling whip and keep your seat swinging in a trot action.
- *There is a big wobble as you attempt to return to shoulder-in.* Ride forward out of the turnaround earlier.

### Combine with other exercises:

Once you are satisfied with the improvement, come out of the turnaround onto a diagonal line and go forward to medium trot. Alternatively, after a step or two of shoulder-in, go into half-pass across the arena to change rein.

# 45. TROT LEG YIELD (OR HALF-PASS) RIDDEN WITH INCREASED SPEED

## Aims:

This remedial exercise is very particular to horses that need to:

- Develop a wider straddling of the legs.
- Achieve greater abduction (opening) of the leading hind leg.

## How to:

1. Start a left leg yield, or left half-pass, across the diagonal from F to H.

2. Once the position is established, increase the size and speed of the trot – use a stronger right-leg aid and a bigger seat action. In rising trot, make a bigger and quicker rise.

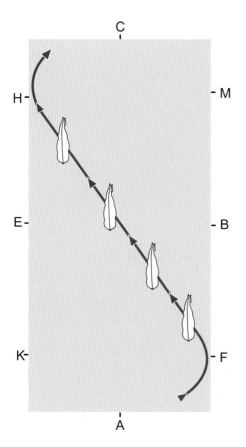

3. The goal is to push the horse sufficiently out of balance that he must reach further across under his body with his right hind leg, OR reach out further with his left hind leg, to re-balance himself depending on which issue you are addressing.

4. Before reaching H, reduce the speed again, back to a normal working tempo.

5. This exercise can also be ridden along the wall in leg yield (see #36) or travers – the wall in front of the horse makes it harder for the horse to avoid the extra movement demanded by this approach.

## Common faults:

- *The horse is reluctant to move faster.* He may need more suppling exercises before he is ready to tackle this exercise. He may also be avoiding the extra demand, which means you must first be certain he is completely sound. Once you have that confirmed, you will need to use firmer aiding to get him to change his established way of going.

- *He breaks into canter.* This may also be a suppleness issue, or avoidance. Use your rising trot in a pronounced fashion, so that you rise and sit very firmly to press the trot rhythm into the saddle with more clarity, and also use more half-halts on the outside rein.

## TOP TIP

It is highly likely that you will only need to ride this exercise in one direction, as the issue is normally specific to just one hind leg – either the weaker one, or the stiffer one, depending on the individual.

# 46. CANTER PLIÉ TO CORRECT AN EXCESSIVE HEEL FIRST ACTION

## Aims:

- To adjust the incorrect footfall of the inside hind when it lands *excessively* heel first.
- The hind hoof should land *slightly* heel before toe, or land flat (depending on which farrier guru you follow), with the weight then rolling forward over the toe. An excessive heel-first landing has the potential to cause soreness/problems in the heel and rear of the hoof, and possible strain to the hind suspensory ligaments.
- From a training point of view this action does not give the desired support to the body weight to enable the horse to spring off the ground with good suspension (jump) in the canter.

## How to:

1. Ride a canter plié – *see* exercise #39.
2. As soon as you start to ride sideways, push the canter a bit faster.
3. To recover balance, the horse will put the hoof down more quickly, which means it will land flatter.
4. Keep the speed up for a little while – for example, ride a 20m circle – after finishing the plié, to get a feel for the extra support before returning to a regular tempo.
5. Repeat at the next centre line.

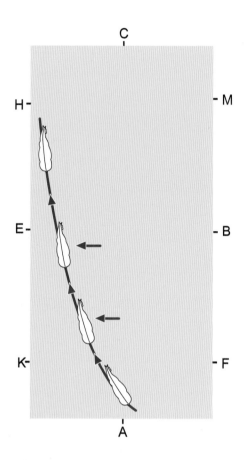

## Common faults:

- *The horse leads too much with the outside shoulder, allowing him to retain his habitual action.* Keep your weight more clearly towards the leading leg, and use your outside rein to partially control the shoulder, but do not hold the shoulder too firmly – it *must* lead, so simply reduce by how much it leads.

## TOP TIP

This exercise is designed to give both you and the horse the experience of a new action. When you feel the old way of moving reassert itself, pop in a plié to remind him you want him to move in the new way, and not the old one.

# DEVELOPMENTAL EXERCISES

## 47. ALTERNATING LARGE AND SMALL CIRCLES

**Walk, trot and canter.**

### Aim:

- To gradually develop collection, especially in horses with big gaits, without the undue mental or physical pressure that can occur when constrained to remain on a circle of a size he finds difficult to achieve with ease.
- The small circle creates collection simply by placing of the hind legs further underneath the horse's body, while the large circle offers a short break from the pressure of the smaller circle.

### How to:

1. Ride a 20m circle at E.
2. At B, ride a single 10m circle, and then return to the 20m circle.
3. At E ride a 10m circle, and then return to the 20m circle.
4. Keep repeating: a single 10m circle followed by half a 20m circle, and then a second 10m circle followed by half a 20m circle.

### Common faults:

- *Loss of rhythm, regularity, or purity of the footfalls of the gait (such as a four-beat canter).* All of these demonstrate that the horse finds it hard to achieve collection. For a short period, make the small circle slightly larger, perhaps 12m, before returning to the 10m size once he can maintain his gait with more ease.
- *The horse falls out, or loses the quarters out, on the 10m circle.* This shows either a resistance to the collecting effect of the small circle, or a lack of suppleness or balance. Be firmer with the outside rein and leg to control the outside of his body and keep the steps aligned to your chosen size.

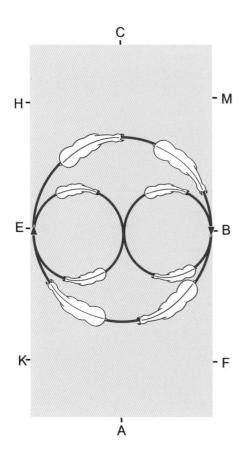

> ### TOP TIP
>
> Monitor the rhythm closely – this tells you whether the horse is achieving collection or not.

# 48. DEVELOPING SHOULDER-IN

**Walk and trot.**

## Aims:

Shoulder-in is the first proper lateral work we teach a horse – the first movement where the horse must bend and move sideways at the same time. It has several purposes, including:

- Straightening (putting the shoulders in front of the haunches).
- Engaging.
- Collecting.
- Lightening the forehand.
- Refining the horse's fine motor controls.

## How to:

As with so many other exercises, shoulder-in should be started in its easier form (shoulder-fore), before progressing to full three-track, or (at advanced level) four-tracks.

1. In the corner by F, ride a 10m circle.
2. As you finish the circle, take one more step as though you were going to continue around another circle.
3. As the horse begins this step, make a half-halt on the outside rein and apply your inside leg in the same moment.
4. This gives you the correct bend and angle for shoulder-in. Continue down the track until you reach B.
5. At B, ride forward onto a 10m circle.
6. At the end of this circle, repeat the same procedure and ride shoulder-in until M.
7. At M, either ride another 10m circle, or proceed around the corner before starting the same sequence at H.

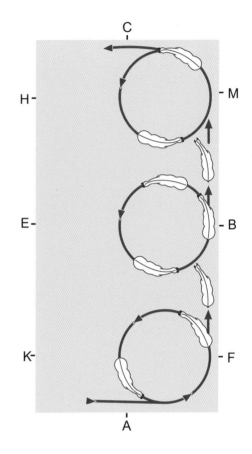

## Common faults:

- *The horse is too straight and crosses his hind legs.* This is leg yield along the wall, and not shoulder-in. Make sure to get a genuine body bend around the 10m circle and then maintain it.
- *The horse falls onto his outside shoulder.* Press the outside rein more firmly against his shoulder.

- *The horse steps off the track.* Use a stronger inside leg aid in coordination with your outside rein half-halts.

---

**TOP TIP**

Once shoulder-in is fully established, the same pattern can be used to develop haunches-in (travers), by keeping the last step of each 10m circle as the first step of the travers.

When you are both confident, try mixing it up – ride shoulder-in for the first half of the long side, and then travers for the second, and vice versa.

# 49. LEG YIELD TO SHOULDER-IN

Trot.

## Aims:

- To use leg yield to confirm to the horse that he must move freely away from the rider's inside leg, before changing the position to shoulder-in, with continued obedience to the inside leg.
- The act of moving the shoulders across in front of the haunches both helps establish the rider's control of the shoulders, and at the same time engages the horse's inside hind leg with resultant lightening of the forehand.

## How to:

1. On the left rein, turn up the centre line at A.
2. Leg yield to the right, as far as the quarter line.
3. At the quarter line, arrest the sideways motion with the outside leg.
4. At the same time, turn the upper body more towards the inside (left), using the outside rein pressed against the neck and shoulder to move the shoulders from the leg yield position (where they are leading towards the track) to the inside of the quarter line, until the horse is in shoulder-in position.
5. Continue up the quarter line in shoulder-in.
6. Turn left at the top, change rein, and repeat on the other rein.

## Common faults:

- *It is a struggle to make the change of position.* Initially, break this down into smaller chunks. At the quarter line, straighten the horse and ride straight on up the quarter line. Once you can do this, ride four or five straight strides and then move the shoulders inwards to shoulder-in position. Gradually reduce the number of straight strides before asking for shoulder-in, until you can move directly from the one position to the other.

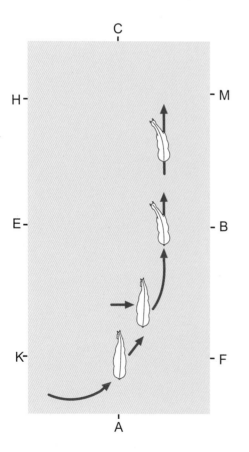

## TOP TIP

To advance this exercise, continue the leg yield as far as the inside track and make the change of position from leg yield to shoulder-in there, before riding the remainder of the inside track in shoulder-in. This is more difficult, because the horse will naturally want to fall towards the track, making the control necessary to change the position more of a challenge.

# 50. SHOULDER-IN WITH TRANSITIONS

Trot.

## Aims:

- To engage the inside hind leg further under the body.
- Strengthen the weight-carrying muscles.
- Increase the flexibility of the joints.
- Lower the croup.
- By training one side at a time, it is possible to target the weaker or less flexible hind leg individually. It is also easier to drive one hind leg under at a time, than both at the same time.
- To teach the rider to collect by driving forward, and not by pulling back on the reins.

## How to:

Transitions can be between paces or within the pace.

1. From the start of one long side ride shoulder-in.
2. Once the angle and balance are established, make a transition. Either to walk, or to medium trot (use your seat to lengthen the strides, while your leg drives the inside hind forward under the horse's body).
3. Maintain shoulder-in throughout. After a few steps, make another transition, either back to trot, or from medium back to working (or collected) trot.
4. At the end of the long side, finish the shoulder-in as normal, and then repeat on the next long side.

## Common faults:

- *Losing the position.* Focus on maintaining the angle and staying in the track while making the transitions. Losing position is the horse's easiest evasion from the engaging effect of this exercise.
- *Struggling to go from walk to trot while in shoulder-in.* Often horses assume canter because of the bend – make sure to keep your weight even in both seat bones when asking for trot.

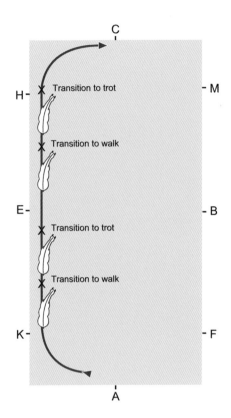

- *Rider pulling back on the reins on the return from medium to working (or collected) trot.* Keep your hands forward, reduce the size of your seat action, and put your inside leg **on** to drive the hind leg under.

## Combine with other exercises:

Use this exercise to improve medium trot and the transitions in and out.

From shoulder-in, straighten onto a short diagonal and go forward to medium trot. When you arrive at the opposite track, turn into the new shoulder-in and recollect by driving the new hind leg under.

# 51. 20m CIRCLE IN SHOULDER-IN, WITH TROT/CANTER AND CANTER/TROT TRANSITIONS

## Aim:

- To develop increased weight carriage of the hind legs in transitions between trot and canter.

## How to:

1. Ride a 20m circle in shoulder-in.
2. Make a transition to canter *from* trot shoulder-in, remaining on the circle.
3. Ride the canter in normal alignment, with the hind feet in the same track as the front feet, for at least half a circle.
4. Develop shoulder-fore in the canter.
5. Make your transition from canter *into* trot shoulder-in – this puts your horse's weight directly over his inside hind leg.

6. Remain in trot shoulder-in on the circle until the rhythm and balance are fully established, and then repeat.

## Common faults:

- *Losing the shape of the circle – falling out or falling in.* This is an evasion of weight carriage on the hind leg. You must monitor the shape of your figure and correct any drift.
- *You struggle to maintain control of the shoulders and/ or haunches.* This indicates that you need a more confirmed inside leg to outside rein connection.
- *He steps forward off the hind leg, making the circle smaller, in one or both of the transitions.* You need to use more inside leg, combined with outside rein half-halts in the moment of transition to keep him on the circle.
- *He hollows in the upward transition.* Ride a more positive forward tempo in the trot to better engage his inside hind leg before asking for the upward transition.

## Combine with other exercises:

Every so often, from the canter, make a transition forward to medium canter for half a circle to refresh the canter, before returning to working canter prior to making the downward transition.

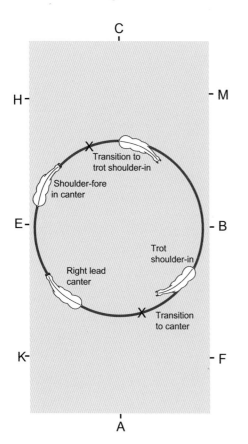

C

H -                                               - M

Transition to
trot shoulder-in

Shoulder-fore
in canter

E -                                               - B

Trot
shoulder-in

Right lead
canter

Transition
to canter

K-                                                - F

A

## TOP TIP

If you struggle with shoulder-in on the circle, focus on keeping the haunches out, but still with your inside leg at the girth – do not move it back. This is an incorrect way of creating shoulder-in, but can be very effective to develop a feel for the exercise if you are new to riding it on the circle.

# 52. COUNTER-FLEXION ON A CIRCLE

**Walk, trot and canter.**

## Aims:

1. To re-confirm understanding of yielding to the bit.
2. To develop an elastic contact – only achievable if both horse and rider are willing to yield to each other.
3. To promote suppleness.

## How to:

1. Ride a 20m circle.
2. Ask for outside flexion by raising your outside hand (to chest level) and taking it across the neck. DO NOT PULL. This lifts the bit into the corner of the mouth, so there must be **no strength** involved, merely a re-positioning of the bit in the horse's mouth.
3. Soften the inside rein contact so the horse can turn his head easily towards the outside.
4. If there is any problem with steering, use occasional touches on the inside rein, opening it towards the middle of the circle.
5. Once the horse yields to the outside rein – he should turn his head to the outside, chew the bit, and lower his head (flex, chew, lower) – **immediately** push your outside hand forwards and down, and scratch him on the withers to confirm he has answered correctly.
6. Put your hands back into their normal positions and apply inside leg to connect him to the outside rein.

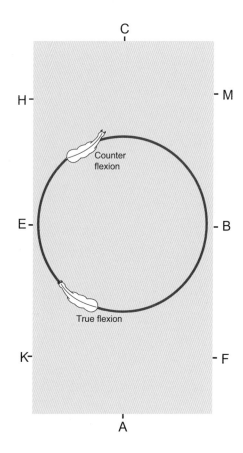

- *The rider does not release the contact immediately.* This is critical to success – be mindful of any small changes in your horse's position and if in doubt, release the contact.

## Common faults:

- *The rider is too strong with the outside hand.* This will only cause stress and argument. **Never** use strength in this exercise.
- *The horse does not yield to the request.* You may not have waited long enough – always wait, do not get stronger. At first, you might need to settle for two of the three answers (flex, chew, lower) in order to encourage. Also try returning to a slower gait.

---

### TOP TIP

If this is a first time trying this exercise, start at halt, then progress to walk, before trying trot.
  **Do not repeat too often.** Twice in a warm-up is sufficient, and only repeat if the horse comes against the hand.

# 53. SHOULDER-IN, RENVERS, SHOULDER-IN

Walk and trot.

## Aims:

- To increase lateral suppleness.
- To help the rider gain more control of both shoulders and haunches at the same time.

## How to:

1. In the 20m × 60m arena, start a long side in left shoulder-in, with your upper body turned to the inside, your weight in your inside seat bone, and your inside leg at the girth.

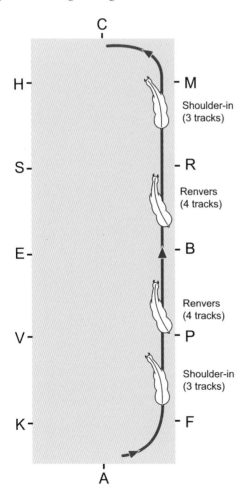

Shoulder-in
(3 tracks)

Renvers
(4 tracks)

Renvers
(4 tracks)

Shoulder-in
(3 tracks)

2. Once the shoulder-in is fully established, change the bend to the right, so you will be in renvers. Do this by reversing your aiding – turn your upper body until you and the horse both face towards the short side of the arena, and put your weight into your right seat bone. Keep the horse's haunches at the wall with your left leg, drawn back into an outside leg position.

3. Once the renvers is fully established, change position again, returning to shoulder-in.

4. If the 20m × 40m arena, make the change of position at B, and then change back to inside bend in time for the corner – you may not have space to do the second shoulder-in, although you can always do that around the short side if you choose.

## Common faults:

- *The horse struggles with the bend change.* Take several steps to achieve this – do not try to make it happen suddenly, or you may pull him out of balance.

- *The horse falls off the track during the change of position to renvers.* Make your weight change and slide your left leg back into outside leg position, pressing it more firmly against his side, slightly *before* changing your upper body position.

## TOP TIP

This exercise is not as easy as it sounds! Start by performing it in walk, and take plenty of time to make the position changes, before trying it at trot. The goal is to make him more supple, and not to make it so difficult that he stiffens up in his efforts to remain in balance.

# EXERCISES TO DEVELOP ENGAGEMENT

## 54. MULTIPLE TRANSITIONS AROUND THE ARENA

### Aims:

- Riding frequent transitions will help to develop a quicker hind leg.
- More prompt reactions to your aids.
- More flexion of the hind leg joints for increased joint suppleness.
- To strengthen the horse's hind-end musculature.

### How to:

1. Going large around the track, start with frequent trot-walk-trot transitions. Do not stay in either walk, or trot, for too many strides before changing gait.
2. Progress to riding trot-halt-trot transitions.
3. When the above are easy, try trot-halt-rein back-trot, but not necessarily all in the same work session! Pick the transitions most appropriate to your horse's training level.

    Other transitions you can perform are:

4. Trot-halt-rein back-medium trot.
5. Collected trot-medium trot-collected trot, and the same in canter.
6. Canter-walk-canter, with or without a change of lead.
7. Canter-halt-canter.
8. Canter-halt-rein back-canter.
9. The point is to use repetition to sharpen the horse's responses, and to exercise the haunch muscles.

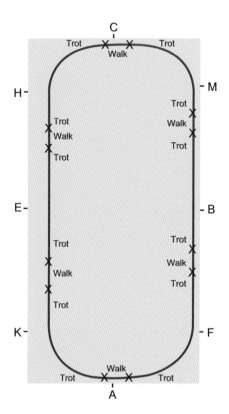

### Common faults:

- *The horse anticipates the transitions and does not wait for your aids.* Stay longer in each gait between transitions – wait until each gait is fully established before asking for the next. This type of horse does not need sharper reactions, but still needs the exercise component for strengthening.

- *There is a lack of reaction to your aids.* For a time or two, be stronger with your driving aids while at the same time pushing your hands forward and losing the contact – in the short term the outline is irrelevant, and the horse must feel he can go forward without any restrictions. Once the responses are better, re-introduce a contact and a normal size of aid.

### TOP TIP

Every time you do not get the reaction you want to your forward driving aids, ride a few quick transitions to reinforce the horse's responses and his attention to you.

# 55. LEG YIELD INWARDS, INTO HALF-CIRCLE

Trot.

## Aims:

- To develop lowering of the croup and engagement in trot.

## How to:

1. You need to know how much sideways the horse is able to travel in leg yield.
2. For this exercise to be of value, the leg yield must arrive on the centre line at either D or G, and not earlier. For example, in a 20m × 40m arena, travelling on the left rein, you will start to leg yield

*away* from the track (leg yield left, in right flexion) somewhere between H and E, to arrive at D.

3. At D, make a half-circle right, allowing the fence to turn the horse so that your rein contact is clearly forward-feeling.
4. As you travel around the half-circle, engage your core muscles and drive the horse with seat and leg but remain at the same speed: the goal is to feel his croup lowering.
5. This is most effective in sitting trot, but can be performed in rising trot if the horse is weak in the back.
6. The leg yield positions the inside hind leg beneath the horse's body prior to the half-circle. The small radius of the half-circle (10m) enables you to further drive the hind leg under, teaching the horse to bend the hind leg joints and lower the croup, achieving engagement and later, collection.

## Common faults:

- *You arrive too early on the centre line.* On repeating, adjust the starting point of your leg yield.
- *The horse does not sit down on the half-circle.* Check your rein contact is not preventing the hind leg from stepping forward. You may need to be more insistent with your weight aids into the saddle and drive a little more with both leg and seat, but without gaining speed.

## Combine with other exercises:

As you come out of the half-circle, go forward on the long side to medium trot. Once this is easy, turn out of the half-circle onto the diagonal to ride the medium.

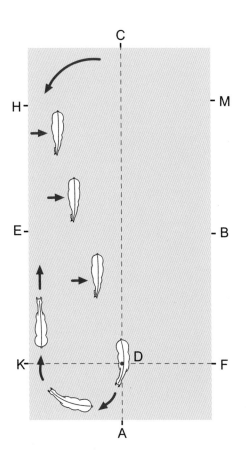

# 56. COLLECT THE CANTER IN PREPARATION FOR A WALK TRANSITION

## Aim:

- To develop direct transitions from canter to walk.
- To strengthen the hindquarters.

## How to:

1. Ride a 10m circle from the track in an arena with a wall or fence alongside the track.
2. Collect the canter in the second half of the circle as you approach the wall. Make repeated small half-halts on the inside rein in each stride, complemented by a push with the inside seat in the same moment to compress the horse between the two aids without stiffening or resistance.
3. In the final stride of the circle *as the horse is facing the wall,* ask for walk with a firm rock back of your *outside* shoulder, ensuring your elbow is against your body so that the movement affects the whole outside of your body, including dropping your outside seat bone firmly down.
4. Immediately the horse walks, relax the aids and allow him to walk away.

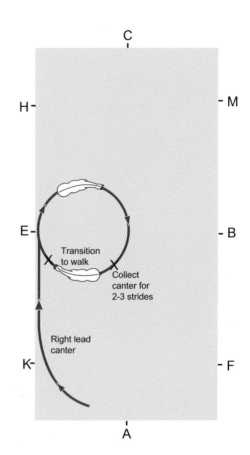

## Common faults:

- *Struggling to achieve collection in the canter.* Review the horse's training level: does he understand how to respond to a half-halt? Is he able to perform a 10m circle in canter with a fair degree of ease? If not, work on these first before returning to this exercise.
- *The downward transition is not direct.* Be firmer with your outside rein aid. Ensure your core tone is firm as you rock your shoulder back or it will not translate clearly through your whole body and down into the saddle.
- *There is a tiny 'dribble' of trot in the transition.* Pretend you are asking for halt instead of walk. Upon achieving walk, quickly relax to permit him to walk forward.

- *The horse jogs instead of walking.* The moment you achieve the transition, drop your reins completely to invite relaxation.

## Combine with other exercises:

This exercise is the first step towards the simple change. Once established, ride the downward transition on the centre line instead of at the wall, then after a few steps of walk ask for the opposite canter lead and half-circle away in the new direction.

# 57. 20m FIGURE OF EIGHT IN CANTER, WITH CHANGE OF LEAD VIA REIN BACK

## Aims:

- By using repetition, and hence developing anticipation, the horse will start to improve his collection into the downward transition from canter to halt.
- The rein back brings the hind legs more under the body for greater engagement in the upward transition to canter and, by alternating leads, the horse is required to pay attention to the rider's aids and react appropriately.

## How to:

1. From X, perform a right-hand 20m circle in right-lead canter.

2. As you approach X again, ask for a transition to halt, aiming to achieve this at X, or no more than a couple of steps later.

3. Rein back four or five steps.

4. Make a transition from rein back directly into left-lead canter and perform a 20m circle left.

5. Upon approaching X, ask again for a halt.

6. Rein back.

7. Make a transition directly into right-lead canter, and perform a 20m circle right.

8. Repeat as many times as necessary until the transitions, both into and out of canter, and into rein back, are satisfactory.

## Common faults:

- *The horse does not halt promptly.* Review your aiding and keep repeating the exercise – repetition works to your advantage in this pattern.
- *The horse is slow to respond to the upward transition aid.* Initially accept a step or two of walk, but then become more positive with your aid, insisting on an immediate departure in canter.
- *The horse tries to pick up the same lead each time.* If your aiding is clear and he still refuses to depart on, for example, the left lead, this might indicate a lack of strength in the left hind leg. Go back to some simpler exercises to target building strength in that hind leg, such as shoulder-in.

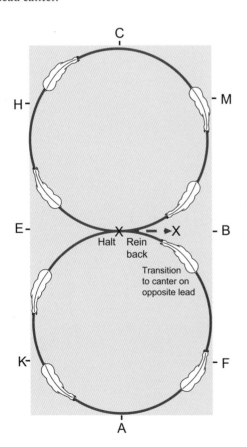

C

H -

- M

E -

X    ►X
Halt   Rein
       back

- B

Transition
to canter on
opposite lead

K -

- F

A

## TOP TIP

If the horse struggles with the direct transition from rein back to canter on a named lead, then walk forward one, or at most two, steps during which you should create a clear position towards the required lead, to remove any confusion.

# 58. FOUR LATERAL POSITIONS ON A CIRCLE

**Walk and trot.**

## Aims:

- A highly suppling exercise.
- Increases engagement.
- Hones the rider's control of both shoulders and haunches.

## How to:

The following sequence is an example: you can move between the various lateral positions in any order you choose.

1. Ride a 20m circle in the centre of the school.
2. Create shoulder-in on this circle.
3. Stay half a circle in shoulder-in, or until the balance is fully established.

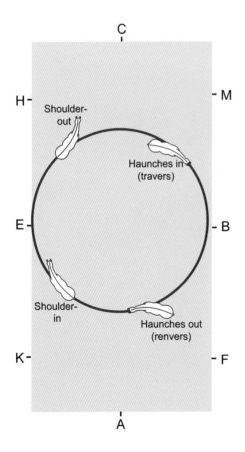

4. Keeping the same bend, move the hindquarters in, to create travers.
5. Ride half a circle, or until the balance and impulsion are established.
6. Change the bend. You will now be in shoulder-out.
7. Ride half a circle, or until the balance is established.
8. Keeping the same bend, move the hindquarters out to put the horse into renvers.
9. Once the renvers is established, change bend and you will be back in shoulder-in.

Vary the order in which you change positions according to what you feel the horse needs. If he struggles with one position (most likely renvers, which is the toughest), then make the next change to an easier position.

Some of the changes are bend changes (for example, renvers to shoulder-in), some are position changes with the same bend (for examples, shoulder-in to travers) and some demand a change of both bend and position at the same time (for example, shoulder-in to shoulder-out, or renvers to travers).

## Common faults:

- *The shape of the circle is lost.* Pay more attention to keeping the horse on the correct line as well as making the lateral position changes.
- *There is a loss of impulsion.* Different horses will find certain positions more challenging: do not stay in the more difficult position for too long; rather make more repetitions for shorter periods.

> ## TOP TIP
>
> For advanced horses, riding these patterns on a smaller circle – down to 10m – yields a big increase in engagement and may amplify the trot cadence, but **do not** attempt a smaller circle until the horse is strong in his haunches.

# 59. WALK PIROUETTE TO CANTER STRIKE OFF

## Aims:

- To use the collecting effect of a walk pirouette to strengthen the horse's hindquarters, by making the transition to canter with his croup lowered.
- To make the horse quicker off the leg in the canter strike off.

## How to:

1. Away from the track, collect the walk and make a few steps of a walk pirouette.
2. When you feel the horse lower his croup, immediately straighten and ask for a canter strike off.
3. Canter just a few steps before returning to walk.
4. Repeat.

## Common faults:

- *The reaction to your leg aid is not prompt.* Once or twice, follow this procedure: before you ask for the canter, throw your hands forward to completely lose the contact, and at the same time, over-aid with your legs and seat. The objective is to startle the horse into a quick response. Outline, and control of the resulting canter, are unimportant in the short term. Once he responds quickly, re-establish contact and normal-sized aids during the transition.

- *The transition is prompt in one direction, but not in the other.* This indicates an inequality in either the strength, or the suppleness, of the two hind legs. If you are absolutely certain the horse is genuinely sound, return to easier strengthening exercises, targeting the less responsive hind leg. *See* exercises #54, #55, #56, and #57.

- *The horse hollows as you ask for canter.* This is a means of evading the extra demand of making the transition with a lowered croup. As you ride around the pirouette steps, take the neck lower with an open inside rein and keep the bend as you ask for canter.

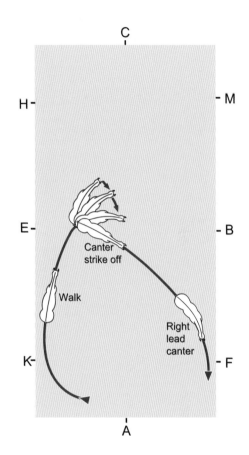

## TOP TIP

Once you are both used to this exercise, you should only need a couple of steps in the walk pirouette before asking for the canter strike off. Repeat several times in quick succession to maximize the strengthening effect of the exercise.

# EXERCISES TO DEVELOP THE MEDIUM GAITS

## 60. 10m CIRCLES INTO, AND OUT OF, MEDIUM TROT AND MEDIUM CANTER

### Aims:

- To develop power and engagement in the medium gaits, and balance and engagement in the return to the working or collected gait.
- The circle prior to the medium helps bring the hind legs under the body in preparation for the transition forward to the bigger steps, while the circle at the end helps to reduce the size of the steps without the rider being tempted to draw back on the reins.

### How to:

1. At the start of a long side, ride a 10m circle, using quick leg aids to increase the activity.
2. Immediately upon returning to the track, ride forward to medium trot (or canter) by swinging your pelvis in a longer sweep along the saddle.
3. At the end of the long side, reduce the size of your pushing seat action and turn onto a 10m circle.
4. Use quick leg aids to encourage the hind legs to step under and keep the activity, while the circle helps you to collect without pulling on the reins.

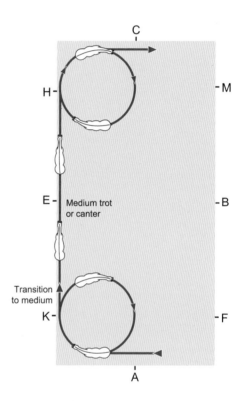

### Common faults:

- *The horse loses activity on the initial 10m circle.* Use a more insistent, quick leg aid to keep him up to tempo.
- *He loses balance in the medium and falls onto the forehand.* Ride a shorter distance in medium before turning onto the end circle. Eventually he will be able to sustain a better balance, as the impulsion gained from the initial circle increases.
- *You find it hard to turn his shoulders onto the end circle.* Step more firmly onto the inside stirrup and exaggerate the turn of your upper body.

Bring both hands towards the inside to push the shoulders onto the circle, making repetitive inward and forward pushes of the rein, rather than keeping them in one position where the horse can lean against them.

### TOP TIP

If the horse struggles to manage a 10m circle, ride this pattern using a slightly larger circle – anything between 12m and 15m – until he is supple enough to produce a 10m circle with ease.

# 61. MEDIUM TROT GOING LARGE AROUND THE ARENA

## Aims:

- To push the horse into big enough steps that he stretches out his front legs to maintain balance. In so doing, he learns to open his shoulders to produce true medium strides.
- Use the short sides to help the horse re-balance and gain more engagement.
- Horses gain psychological support from working alongside a fence, so using the outside track will give you a better chance of finding medium strides than riding across the diagonal.
- It will *not* work with a horse that has limited shoulder action by virtue of conformation.

## How to:

1. In rising trot, ride large around the perimeter of the arena.
2. Make the corners shallow, as if you were riding half a 20m circle at each end of the arena.
3. On the short sides, use your legs to create impulsion.
4. On the long sides, make a bigger rise by swinging your hips higher, and in a longer forward sweep.
5. Do not reduce the stride or try to rebalance the horse on the next short side – the pattern will do that for you. Use more leg again and build up to progressively bigger steps as the exercise continues.
6. Once you have achieved some genuinely longer steps, praise the horse and give him a short rest break before repeating on the other rein.

## Common faults:

- *The trot loses rhythm, or breaks into canter.* Return to a smaller trot, change the rein on the diagonal, and try again in the other direction.
- *The horse falls onto the forehand and paddles with his front legs.* You probably asked for the medium steps too suddenly – make the increases more gradual.

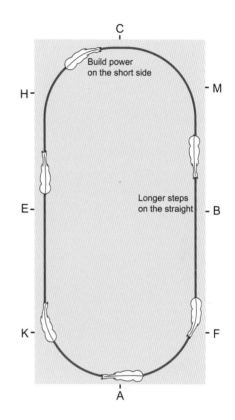

- *No longer strides are achieved.* Provided you have given this exercise enough time to work, and still not had a positive result, try a different technique instead.

## TOP TIP

If it is working well, and the strides are becoming long without an increase in speed or a loss of balance, then maintain them across the diagonal and continue increasing on the other rein without stopping.

# 62. MEDIUM TRANSITIONS ALL AROUND THE ARENA

Trot and canter.

## Aims:

• To improve the horse's reactions and strength by riding frequent transitions without insisting on maintenance of the medium gait following the transitions.

## How to:

1. Anywhere around the track, in working trot or canter, ask for a forward reaction to bigger, more impulsive steps. You want a prompt reaction – the quality of the following steps is not important at this stage.

2. As soon as the horse has reacted, after two or three bigger steps (initially, even quicker steps are acceptable), allow the gait to return to a regular working speed and rhythm. *Do not* ask for this return using the reins, simply keep your legs quiet and *allow* it to happen. A nervous horse might take longer than a lazy horse; let him do it at his own speed.

3. Once working speed and rhythm are established, repeat.

4. This can, and should, be done all around the track, and not just on the long sides. In a short arena aim for a minimum of two reactions to a long side, with one on the short side. Ask in corners as well. The goal is that the horse learns to react to your aids, and not that he assumes medium gaits will only happen in certain positions in the arena, such as the long side, or the diagonal.

## Common faults:

• *In trot, the horse loses rhythm, or breaks into canter.* Initially, this is not an issue – the important thing is the reaction to your aids. As you repeat, start to insist on a clearer rhythm with exaggeratedly firm rising and sitting in the rhythm you want, and not the one the horse offers.

• *There is no reaction.* Be firmer – use stronger leg aids backed up with a schooling stick.

• *The horse becomes anxious.* Use smaller aids, and take more time to establish the regular working trot between repetitions.

## TOP TIP

Once the reactions are eager, and the rhythm in subsequent steps improved, start to sustain the medium steps for longer periods, eventually building up to a full long side or diagonal.

# 63. SHOULDER-IN TO MEDIUM TROT, TO SHOULDER-IN

Trot.

## Aims:

- To develop medium trot by starting from the shoulder-in, which engages the inside hind leg to a greater degree than a straight line or a turn.
- To harness the extra impulsion created by the medium.
- To teach riders to *drive forward into collection* at the end of medium, and not to pull back.

## How to:

1. Begin the long side in shoulder-in.
2. Once the balance and engagement are established, straighten the horse back onto the track. Do *not* change bend as you do so, but keep the clear connection to the outside rein.
3. Ride immediately forward into medium trot.
4. Once the medium is established, or around two thirds of the way along the long side, return to the shoulder-in position. *Do not* try to collect the horse first, but push the shoulders inwards and drive the hind leg under to create true collection.

## Common faults:

- *The horse loses balance when moving from shoulder-in to straight.* Practise moving the horse in and out of shoulder-in without attempting medium trot, until he can maintain balance.
- *The medium trot drops onto the forehand after a few steps.* Return to shoulder-in sooner, aiming to do so *before* the balance tips downwards. Gradually, with repetition, you will be able to add more steps in medium before the balance is compromised.
- *The horse tries to slow down going into the second shoulder-in.* Drive more strongly to maintain the forward impetus. *Do* allow the strides to become smaller as the shoulder-in progresses, but do not accept a reduction in stride *before* the shoulder-in is established.

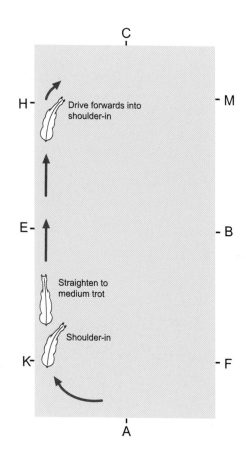

C

H –                                    – M

Drive forwards into shoulder-in

E –                                    – B

Straighten to medium trot

Shoulder-in

K –                                    – F

A

## TOP TIP

Your legs in the shoulder-in create the necessary impulsion. Release it into the bigger strides by using a longer sweep of your pelvis along the saddle and *stop using your legs*. As you drive into the second shoulder-in, reduce the size of your seat action while driving positively with your inside leg in order to gather the inside hind beneath the horse's body.

# 64. SHOULDER-IN TO MEDIUM TROT ON THE DIAGONAL

## Aims:

- To use the engaging effect of shoulder-in to prepare the medium trot.

## How to:

1. Ride shoulder-in on the long side from F – B.

2. From B, *straighten* onto the short diagonal towards H by closing your outside rein and outside leg.

3. As soon as the horse is straight, ask for medium trot by using a bigger swinging action of your seat but without leg aids.

4. As you approach H, reduce the size of your seat action and close your legs to ask the horse to bring his hind legs forward and under, and go into the corner with engagement and bend.

5. If the trot is balanced and rhythmic by the time you reach M, repeat with shoulder-in until B, and medium across the short diagonal to K.

6. In the 20m × 40m arena you will only get a few steps of medium so, if possible, ride this exercise in a 20m × 60m arena for the best result.

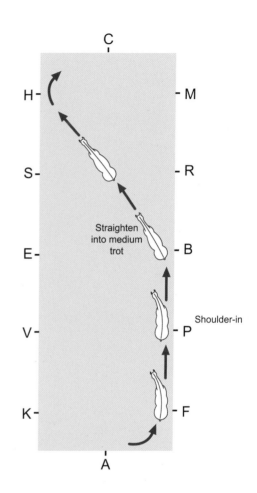

## Common faults:

- *The horse breaks into canter as you ask for medium.* You need to be firmer about straightness before asking for medium, even if achieving straightness takes a step or two longer than ideal.

- *The medium steps are hurried.* Make sure to swing your seat at the speed *you* want, rather than that offered by the horse.

- *There is a loss of rhythm as you enter the corner after the medium.* Next time, ask for the return to working or collected trot a bit sooner, and make sure your seat (either rising or sitting) is moving in a clear trot rhythm in the saddle, regardless of what your horse does.

## TOP TIP

If you want to cover more distance in the medium trot, ride shoulder-in around the short side and just a step or two down the long side, before turning onto a diagonal line towards the opposite quarter marker.

# 65. HALF ROUND IN MEDIUM CANTER

## Aim:

- To develop both the pushing, and the carrying, power of the haunches.
- To improve reactions both into, and back from, medium canter.

## How to:

1. Ride a 20m circle at one end of the arena.
2. Ride the closed side (alongside the wall) in working or collected canter (depending on the horse's training level).

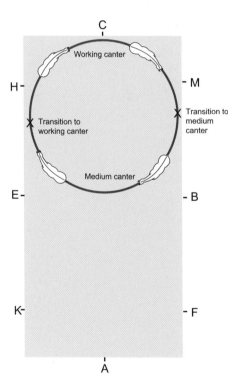

3. As you leave the wall, make a transition to medium canter and ride the open side in medium canter.
4. As you approach the wall (closed side), make a transition to working or collected canter.
5. Repeat several times.
6. By doing this exercise repetitively, the horse will start to anticipate the transitions (in a good way) and so help you to ride them with smaller and smaller aids for greater responses.

## Common faults:

- *A lack of reaction in either transition.* You may need to be a little sharper with your aids a time or two until the repetitive nature of the exercise starts to work for you.
- *The medium canter is not big enough.* Ensure you are pushing along with a sufficiently large (but not fast) motion of your hips to make it clear that you want longer steps.
- *The horse falls out on the open side.* Use exaggerated turning aids, pushing the outside rein against the shoulder, and using the outside leg more firmly.
- *There is no body bend/the horse leans to the inside during the medium canter.* Create more bend with your inside leg *before* you ask for the medium strides.

## Combine with other exercises:

Use the reaction to medium for a half-circle to refresh the canter after any collecting exercise.

# 66. MEDIUM STRIDES TO HALT

Trot and canter.

## Aims:

*N. B. This exercise is only appropriate for a horse with an established understanding of how to engage in downward transitions.*

- For an experienced rider with a keen horse, this exercise improves the promptness of the transition back from medium strides without the rider needing to use strong rein aids.
- To bring the hind legs forward under the body for greater engagement.

## How to:

For this exercise, you need an arena with a solid fence, or a wall, enclosing the appropriate corner.

In trot:

1. Establish the trot with good impulsion on the FAK short side of the arena.
2. Ride medium trot across the KXM diagonal.
3. Just before M, start to collect by reducing the size of your seat action in the saddle, and making half-halts on the reins.
4. At M, start asking for halt, and instead of turning the corner, ride straight ahead.
5. Halt, facing the fence.
6. Stand still in the corner, facing the fence, and praise the horse to reassure him.
7. Proceed out of the corner at walk, possibly on a long rein to help relaxation.

In canter:

1. Activate the canter on the KAF short side.
2. Ride medium canter down the FM long side of the arena.
3. Just before M, collect the canter.
4. Do not turn the corner. Halt, facing the fence, and praise him.
5. Proceed out of the corner at walk, possibly on a long rein to help relaxation.

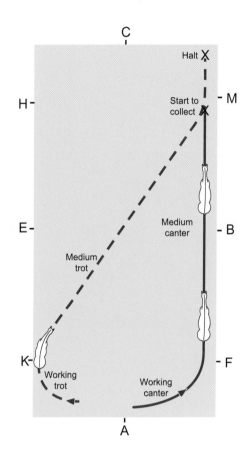

## Common faults:

- *The horse tries to turn the corner instead of halting.* Use your inside leg and outside rein more positively to keep him straight, and allow the fence to do the job of stopping him.

## TOP TIP

This exercise rarely needs more than one repetition to have a positive result.

# EXERCISES TO DEVELOP HALF-PASS

## 67. RENVERSÉE – TURN AROUND THE FOREHAND IN RENVERS POSITION

Walk only.

### Aims:

- A highly suppling exercise.
- To teach the rider the use of the outside rein to move the hindquarters towards the direction of the horse's bend.
- To increase the straddling of the hind legs in half-pass.

### How to:

1. Walk on a very small circle – around 3–5m – on the left rein.
2. Create a counter (right) flexion by taking your right rein into the horse's shoulder, and your left rein towards the middle of the circle.
3. Put your weight more on your *right* seat bone and stirrup.
4. With your left leg, push the haunches towards the right until the hindquarters are moving in a larger circle around the forehand.
5. To gain more displacement of the haunches, or crossing of the hind legs, make small, repeated half-halts on the left rein *away* from the shoulder, that is, towards the middle of the small circle.
6. Once you achieve good crossing of the hind legs with an easy right flexion, turn away out of the circle onto the right rein and repeat in the opposite direction.

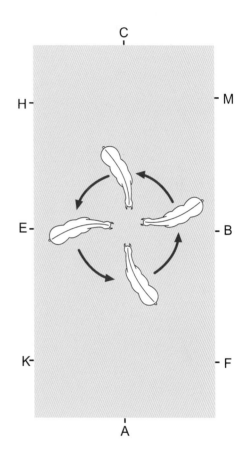

### Common faults:

- *Horse and rider become tense – the horse may come against the hand, and may even stop moving at all or possibly run backwards.* This means you are being too strong with your aids. Give smaller, more frequent aids, especially with the reins, rather than stronger ones.

- *The horse struggles with moving the hind quarters over.* Check that your weight is towards the inside of the bend.

### Combine with other exercises:

Once you can perform the exercise with ease, try coming out of it directly into a half-pass – the horse's position and the aids you are employing for renversée are exactly the same as for half-pass, simply performed on a circle instead of a straight line. It can also be put into the middle of a walk half-pass to make the horse more mobile and obedient to the aids.

# 68. TRAVERS AGAINST A DIAGONAL LINE OF POLES

Walk, trot and canter.

## Aims:

- To introduce the concept of travelling sideways with bend in the direction of travel. As a lesser degree of bend is required for travers than for half-pass, this is a good introductory exercise.
- The goal is for horse and rider to learn to prioritise *forwards* travel over sideways.

## How to:

1. Lay a line of poles across the diagonal of the arena, preferably raised off the ground so that the horse is less likely to step over them (*see* diagram). The line of poles represents the track, simply placed in a different position within the arena.
2. Ride travers along the track. The horse's head and neck should be looking straight along the track, with the haunches displaced to the inside.
3. Have your weight towards the *inside* of the bend, that is, towards the direction of travel.
4. Next, imagine the line of poles to be the track, and ride travers at exactly the same angle along that line.
5. Once this is easy, gradually increase the body bend while keeping the head and neck aligned to the straight line. Eventually this will become a half-pass.

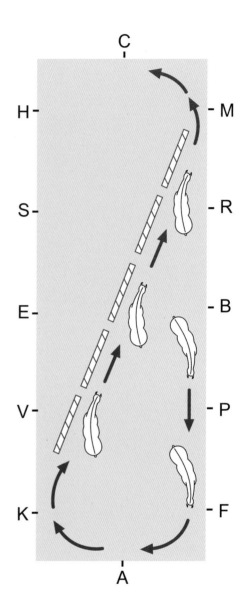

## Common faults:

- *The horse struggles with the bend, especially in one direction.* Work more on the horse's basic suppleness.
- *The horse does not look straight along the line.* You are probably focusing too much on pushing the hindquarters to the side, instead of positioning the front end. Keep the alignment of head and neck to the line, and only displace the hindquarters as far as possible *without* losing the front-end position.
- *The rider's weight slips to the outside of the saddle.* Usually caused by the rider collapsing one side of their body in an effort to push the horse sideways. Use mirrors, or someone on the ground, to correct your body position.

---

### TOP TIP

Travers on the diagonal line *is* a baby half-pass, and should always be used to introduce young horses and inexperienced riders to the movement, before attempting the finished half-pass positioning.

# 69. SHOULDER-IN – HALF-PASS – SHOULDER-IN

Walk and trot. Can also be ridden in canter by substituting shoulder-fore for shoulder-in.

### Aims:

- To help develop the correct positioning and bend in half-pass.
- To alternately engage first the inside, and then the outside, hind legs. This is of gymnastic value, and offers the horse and rider a means of developing half-pass when the horse struggles to maintain bend for long distances.

### How to:

1. Start at K on the right rein, and ride shoulder-in on the track.
2. Once shoulder-in is established (balance, angle, engagement, and acceptance of the body bend) start a right half-pass.
3. When the bend starts to lessen, or the horse loses impulsion, return to shoulder-in position and ride parallel to the track.
4. Once shoulder-in is re-established, return to riding half-pass.
5. Repeat as often as you need, across the width of the arena.
6. You may ride only a few metres in each position – it is up to you to respond to what the horse struggles with, and make the change.

### Common faults:

- *The horse loses balance in the change of position.* Try riding the exercise in walk first, to make it easier for the horse to remain in balance, before trying it in trot.
- *The horse falls onto the outside shoulder during shoulder-in.* Take care as you change the position to move the horse's shoulders to the right – do not just push sideways with your right leg as this may push him out of balance.
- *The hindquarters trail in half-pass.* At first, this is not a critical issue. As you increase the horse's suppleness, you will be able to keep a position more parallel to the track by creating more bend in the horse's body.

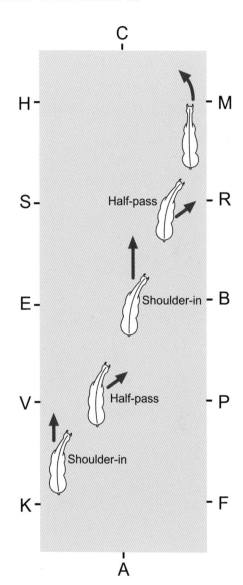

## TOP TIP

On the horse's stiffer side, this exercise challenges body suppleness. On the hollow/more flexible side, it is particularly useful for preventing the hindquarters from leading in half-pass.

# 70. HALF-PASS TO RENVERS TO SHOULDER-IN

**Walk and trot.**

## Aims:

- To teach the rider how to finish a half-pass. Less experienced riders often fail to finish a half-pass, letting the position fade so that the last couple of steps become a vague diagonal line with the shoulders arriving at the track well in advance of the haunches.

- Whilst the shoulders *must* fractionally lead *during* half-pass, in a correctly finished half-pass both shoulders and haunches arrive at the track at the same time, with the bend maintained until that is achieved. To do this, the haunches must move more sideways in the last two steps, and this exercise teaches both the technique and the feel by using a slight exaggeration of the finished movement.

## How to:

1. On the right rein at A turn down the centre line.
2. Ride half-pass right towards B.
3. At the inside track, stop the shoulder from moving sideways with half-halts on the outside rein.
4. Maintain the right bend, and move the haunches out to meet the track, putting your horse into renvers.
5. After a few steps of renvers, change the bend. You will now be in shoulder-in left.

## Common faults:

- *Losing control of the shoulders.* For a few times, simply stop the half-pass at the inside track and ride straight, instead of allowing the horse to travel all the way to the track.

- *Changing the bend too early.* The point of this exercise is to keep the horse in the half-pass bend until the quarters are fully in the track. Wait until the hind legs are both in the track before changing bend.

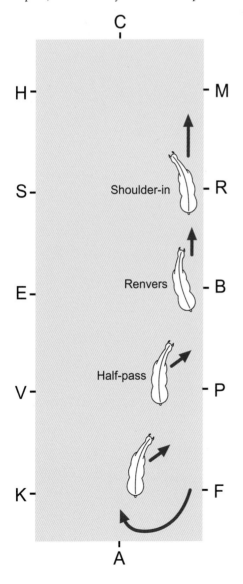

## TOP TIP

Once you can do this, in the last two steps of your half-pass simply create the feeling of the above exercise but without completely stopping the shoulders at the inside track. Your goal is to arrive at the track in the *tiniest* hint of shoulder-fore *to the new direction.*

# 71. HALF-PASS TO RENVERS, TO HALF-PASS

Walk and trot.

## Aims:

- To deepen the crossing of the hind legs by improving the horse's body bend, and the rider's control of the haunches.
- This exercise is most appropriate to a horse that tends to trail the hindquarters in half-passes.

## How to:

1. On the right rein, turn onto the centre line at A.
2. Ride half-pass right from the centre line towards B.
3. When the horse's shoulders arrive on the inside track, take the haunches ahead until they reach the track, that is, renvers position.
4. Continue along the track in renvers.
5. Turn onto the centre line at C, maintaining the renvers position during the turn.
6. Upon arrival on the centre line, begin a new right half-pass.

## Common faults:

- *The horse struggles to maintain the bend.* This is one of the points this exercise is designed to address. Keep as much bend as possible without causing resistance or impacting the rhythm, and continue riding the pattern. With repetition over a period of time (which may be days or even weeks) the horse's ability to bend within the half-pass will improve.
- *The quarters lead in the second half-pass.* This may well happen if the horse finds the renvers fairly easy. In this case, begin the new half-pass before fully completing the turn onto the centre line, that is, with the shoulders *slightly* in advance of the hindquarters.

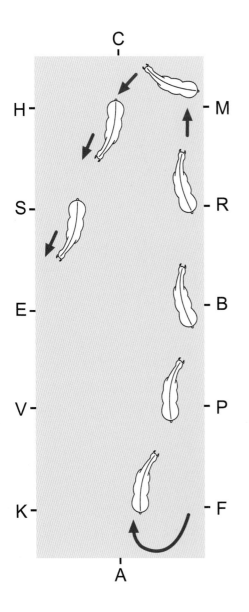

## TOP TIP

Repeat this exercise several times for maximum effect. Once horse and rider become accustomed to the demands of the pattern, greater relaxation and confidence from both parties will yield greater results in terms of depth of crossing of the legs – one of the measures of the quality of a half-pass.

# 72. HALF-PASS TO LEG YIELD, TO HALF-PASS

Walk, trot and canter.

## Aims:

- To further supple and teach the horse to take bigger sideways steps in half-pass, by opening (stretching) the shoulders and increasing the crossing using the simpler positioning of leg yield.
- Much of the quality of a correctly positioned half-pass is measured by the ease with which the horse takes the sideways steps, provided that the rhythm and quality of the gait remains the same before, during and after the movement.

## How to:

1. Begin a right half-pass from K, aiming for the full diagonal, to arrive at M.
2. At the quarter line, change the horse's position to leg yield and ask for the maximum size of sideways step that he is capable of.
3. Just before the three-quarter line, change the positioning (bend) back to half-pass, and endeavour to maintain the same amount of sideways travel as achieved in the leg yield.

## Common faults:

- *The horse loses balance during the changes of position.* Initially try riding this exercise along the wall, that is, travers to leg yield to travers. The wall in front of him will help him to stay in a more consistent balance. Once he can do this with ease, ride the exercise on the diagonal.
- *The horse struggles with the bend changes.* Return to more supling work, particularly changes between bend in lateral work – see exercises #53 and #58.
- *The size of sideways steps does not increase.* Be more demanding of the sideways reach during the leg yield. If this does not yield results, return to working on leg yields at steeper angles with bigger crossing before trying this exercise again.

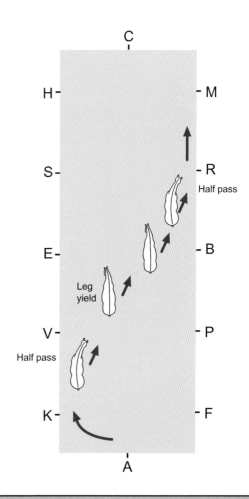

## TOP TIP

Before attempting this, or similar exercises to increase range of motion, be certain that the horse is capable of performing the basic movement with relative ease, that is a rhythm and cadence that are consistent before, during and after the movement (half-pass, in this case), and that he is capable of the required bend without resistance or stiffening.

# 73. HALF-PASS TO MEDIUM, TO HALF-PASS

Trot and canter.

## Aims:

- To increase the power, quality and expression of the gait within the half-pass.

## How to:

1. In a collected gait, begin a right half-pass from K, aiming to arrive at M.
2. At the quarter line, straighten onto the diagonal and go forward to medium.
3. Just before the three-quarter line, regain the half-pass positioning (even if the hindquarters trail a little) and keep the size of the strides until M.
4. Over time, the horse will gain sufficient balance and suppleness to achieve better positioning without losing the extra power. In the earlier stages the goal is to teach acceptance of the bigger strides within the half-pass, so a less than parallel position will still be productive.

## Common faults:

- *In trot, the horse breaks into canter when you ask for medium trot.* Take more care to straighten fully before asking for medium.
- *In trot, the horse breaks into canter when you ask for the return to half-pass position.* Be very clear with your seat action that you are asking for trot, and not allow your seat to take up a canter rhythm.
- *You struggle to return to the half-pass position.* As well as taking your outside leg further back, use more half-halts on the outside rein to bring the hindquarters into place.
- *There is a loss of impulsion as you return to half-pass.* Be more insistent with your inside leg to maintain impulsion, as well as using your outside leg to displace the hindquarters to the side.
- *The horse loses balance in the medium trot and is too much on the shoulders when you try to return to half-pass.* At first, use either a slightly smaller increase in stride length, or a shorter distance in the medium, until he can maintain balance for longer.

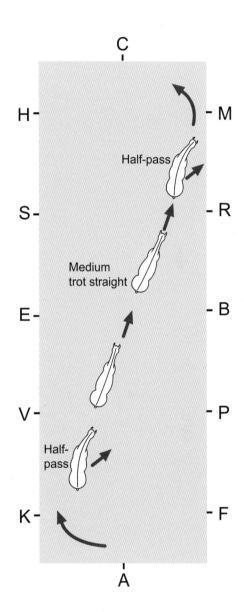

## TOP TIP

Wait to try this exercise until the horse is well-engaged in a regular half-pass – to fully benefit he needs to have a fair degree of self-carriage.

# 74. HALF-PASS IN, LEG YIELD OUT

Walk, trot and canter.

## Aims:

- To improve suppleness and confidence in half-pass.
- To exercise alternate hind legs within the same exercise.
- To improve response to your sideways displacing leg aids.

- This exercise is also good preparation for the zigzag, when you will go from one half-pass to the other.

## How to:

1. From F half-pass left towards X.
2. At the quarter line (before reaching the centre line), straighten and then move his shoulders to the *right*, and return to the track in leg yield (or in canter, a plié).
3. Keep your weight in the left seat bone throughout.
4. Repeat from H towards X.
5. As this becomes easier, aim to travel further across the arena before making the change from half-pass to leg yield, with the aim eventually of making the change of direction *at* X. This is obviously easier to achieve in the 60m arena, but the pattern can be ridden in both sizes of arena.

## Common faults:

- *The half-pass lacks bend.* Ride around the preceding short side in shoulder-in to establish the bend, or ride a 10m circle before starting the half-pass. As soon as you start to lose the bend or balance in the half-pass, make an immediate change into the leg yield.

- *You struggle to get the leg yield to travel sideways.* Make sure you have moved the shoulders back towards the track – if the haunches are leading, the horse will not be able to move sideways.

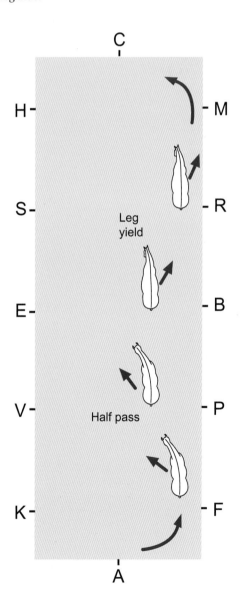

Leg yield

Half pass

## TOP TIP

Try riding this exercise the other way around – leg yield left away from the track, F to X, and then move the shoulders towards the right, and ride half-pass right back to the track. Eventually, ride half-pass left to half-pass right – two legs of a zigzag.

# 75. ALTERNATING SHOULDER-FORE AND TRAVERS TO PREPARE HALF-PASS

Walk, trot, and canter.

## Aims:

- By alternately displacing the shoulders, and then the hindquarters, all the controls of the horse's body are re-confirmed prior to positioning for the half-pass.
- Both exercises also increase engagement, developing a higher degree of collection to make the half-pass easier, or more powerful, depending on the training level.

## How to:

1. On the left rein, ride shoulder-in (shoulder-fore, in canter) from F to B.
2. At B, take the shoulders back to the wall while keeping the bend, and move the hindquarters in, into travers position.
3. Ride travers from B to M.
4. Keep the collection and balance around the short side.
5. Ride half-pass from H to X and proceed down the centre line.
6. At A turn left and repeat.

   If you wish to change the rein:
1. Following the shoulder-in/shoulder-fore and the travers, turn onto the centre line at C.
2. Ride half-pass left to B.
3. In canter, perform a change of lead at F.
4. Repeat on the right rein, starting with shoulder-in/shoulder-fore from K to E.

## Common faults:

- *There is a loss of balance during the position change from shoulder-in/shoulder-fore to travers.* Instead of making a direct change of position, ride a 10m

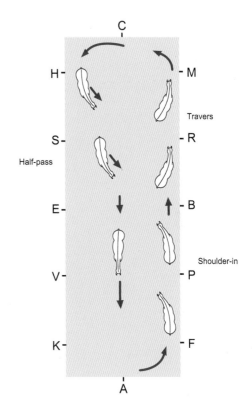

circle at B to finish the shoulder-in, and start the travers from the end of the circle.
- *The horse loses balance on the short side.* Ride shoulder-in (or shoulder-fore in canter) around the short side preceding the half-pass.

## TOP TIP

If the horse is not engaged or collected enough at the end of the travers, repeat the sequence down the next long side before attempting the half pass.

# 76. CANTER PLIÉ TO SHOULDER-FORE, INTO CANTER HALF-PASS

## Aims:

- To exercise both hind legs individually within the one exercise: the inside hind carries the weight in the plié and the shoulder-fore, while the outside hind carries in the half-pass.
- The first part of the exercise sets up the bend and position for the half pass.

If ridden in the 20m × 40m arena, start the exercise from the three-quarter line to give you enough space.

## How to:

1. In left-canter from A, ride a plié outward to the track.
2. At the track, move the shoulders slightly inward, into shoulder-fore.
3. Once shoulder-fore is established, ride half-pass left to the centre line.
4. At C, turn left.

## Common faults:

- *The position change from plié to shoulder-fore is a struggle.* Maintain more control of the outside shoulder during the plié, then the shoulders will be carrying less of the body weight and be easier to manoeuvre.
- *The horse clings to the track, making it difficult to start the half-pass.* Take the shoulders more inwards off the track and put more weight into the inside stirrup before asking for the half-pass.

## Combine with other exercises:

Follow this pattern with a medium canter down the long side to refresh the canter before repeating again from A. If the canter lacks balance at the end of the medium, ride a 15m circle at A to engage the hind legs more under the body before repeating.

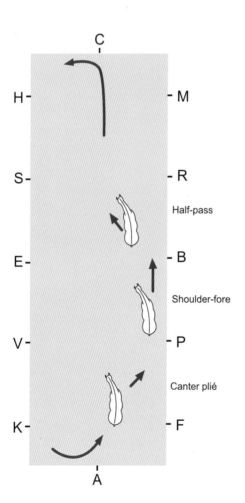

# 77. COUNTER CHANGE OF HAND (ZIGZAG) WITH CIRCLES

Walk, trot and canter.

## Aims:

- An easy introduction to zigzags, using two 10m circles in the middle to allow plenty of time for ease of making the bend change.

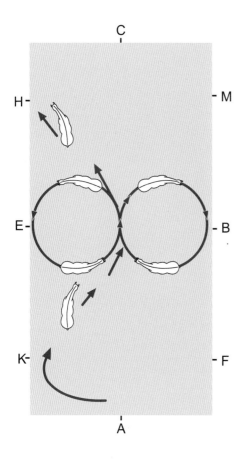

## How to:

1. Half-pass right from K to X.
2. At X, ride a 10m circle right.
3. On returning to X, ride a 10m circle left.
4. X to H, half-pass left.
5. If performed in canter, make either a flying change, or a simple change, between the two 10m circles.

## Common faults:

- *The horse struggles with the bend change between the two small circles.* Ride patterns to address this issue without the half-passes, before returning to this exercise. *See exercises #6, #7, #21, and #26.*
- *There is a loss of rhythm or balance during the bend change.* Stay as many times round the second circle as you need to re-establish the way of going before riding the second half-pass.

## Combine with other exercises:

Once this becomes easy, you will be ready to take the next step towards the zigzag: at X, change from the right half-pass directly into the left circle, and then left half-pass.

The final step will be to remove the preparatory circle altogether, and go directly from right half-pass, to left bend, into left half-pass – a true zigzag.

# EXERCISES TO DEVELOP WALK PIROUETTES

## 78. TRANSITIONS MEDIUM TO COLLECTED WALK, WITH GROUND POLES

### Aims:

- To confirm acceptance of the aids in the transition to collected walk.
- To teach the horse to maintain activity in collected walk by using poles to create higher, shorter steps.
- Preparation for walk pirouettes.

### How to:

1. Position four or six ground poles (use even numbers for equal lifting of both hind legs) as in the diagram, closer together than for medium walk: 1m or less apart.

2. In medium walk, ride a 15m square (#22) away from the tracks.

3. Following the corner preceding the ground poles, collect the walk: reduce the size of your seat action, make repeated small half-halts, and maintain speed and activity with quick, but not strong, leg aids while you walk over the poles.

4. At the next corner return to medium walk: relax the contact a little forward to allow the frame to lengthen, swing your seat in a slightly bigger action, and relax your legs using them less, or not at all.

5. After the next corner, again collect the walk and walk over the poles.

6. Repeat often until the horse accepts the collecting aids and maintains the speed and activity of the walk throughout.

### Common faults:

- *The horse resists the contact as you collect.* Use smaller, more frequent rein aids. Too strong a contact will stiffen the frame, which blocks the hind legs from stepping under.

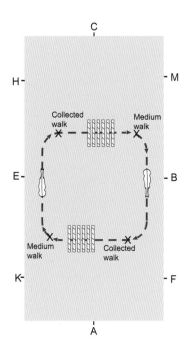

- *The walk slows down in collection.* Use quicker, insistent leg aids to maintain speed and activity. Back your leg up with a schooling whip if necessary, making quick, small taps.

- *The horse swings his quarters into collection.* Either you are using too strong a contact (*see* above), or the horse is physically stiff in the back or hind leg joints. First check there are no physical problems, and if not, do more topline suppling exercises (#29, #30, #31, #32) and return to this pattern with less demand by placing the poles slightly further apart.

---

### TOP TIP

Once this is performed well, remove the poles and ask for collection in the same place on the square.

# 79. DEVELOPING WALK PIROUETTES ON A SQUARE

## Aims:

- To teach the horse to bend the hind legs joints, and as a consequence, to lower the croup – that is, engagement and collection.

## How to:

1. Ride a 20m square (#22).
2. On the corner of the square leaving the track, ride a quarter pirouette.
3. Put your weight in your inside seat bone.
4. Ask for a little inside bend with gentle vibrations on the inside rein.
5. Use your inside leg at the girth to promote activity.
6. Draw your outside leg back *from the hip*, to prevent the haunches from swinging out as you turn.
7. Turn the shoulders with the outside rein pushing *forward* and pressed onto the neck and shoulder.
8. A quarter-turn is only about two steps, so be ready to ride forward (inside leg) by the second turning step.
9. As the exercise becomes easier, reduce the square to 15m ridden away from the tracks, and place a quarter-pirouette on every corner.

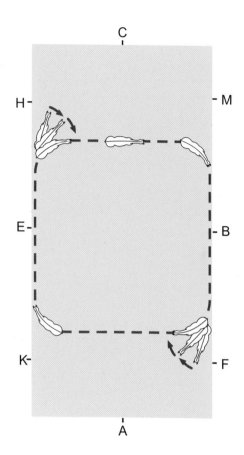

## Common faults:

- *The hindquarters swing out.* Check the horse's responses to your outside leg, and then be more demanding with that aid as you turn the shoulders.
- *The horse overturns.* Be quicker with your inside leg to ride forward out of the turn – start using it as soon as the shoulders have begun to turn.
- *You lose the inside bend.* Make sure you are pushing your outside hand forward (to allow the bend) as well as against the neck to turn the horse.
- *You slip, or the horse pushes you, onto the outside of the saddle.* Step repeatedly to the inside in an exaggerated fashion.

- *The horse loses activity, or loses the walk sequence.* Use your inside leg to keep the activity and, in the early stages, make the turns a bit bigger.

### TOP TIP

Remember the purpose of a pirouette is to lower the croup – being on the forehand causes many of the above issues. Whilst keeping him on the bit, do not let the poll drop – if necessary, make small, quick, upward half halts to discourage this.

# 80. DEVELOPING WALK PIROUETTES ON A CIRCLE

## Aims:

- See also the previous exercise.
- Developing pirouettes on the circle is a good way for both horse and rider to learn the correct order of priorities in terms of the way of going, when presenting pirouettes: forward, bent and active.

## How to:

1. Ride a 10m circle in walk.
2. Develop haunches in around the circle.
3. Keep the forehand aligned to (bent around) and travelling around the circle as your priority, with displacement of the haunches secondary.
4. Ride around this pattern until keeping the position and the activity is easy, and then ride out of it as a reward.
5. When the horse has had a break, return to the pattern. This time, reduce the size of the circle for a few steps, keeping the same priorities.
6. When you feel the weight transfer to the horse's haunches, stay in the pattern for a few steps before enlarging the circle.
7. Play with the size of the circle, reducing and enlarging it, until you are fully in control of every step.
8. Now you are ready to ride a correct pirouette.
9. Repeat on the other rein.

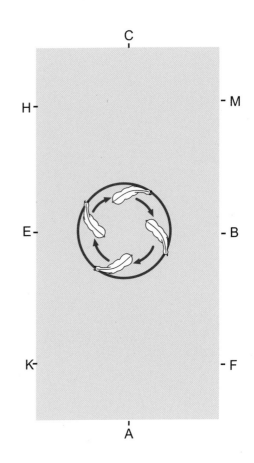

## Common faults:

- *See* the corrections detailed in the previous exercise.
- *The haunches move sideways quicker than the shoulders, so you cannot turn the forehand.* Go back to riding the circle without haunches in, before re-introducing a little haunches in, along with more use of your inside leg to maintain the forward travel instead of excess sideways displacement.
- *The horse comes above the bit.* Remember to *push* the horse around the circle with forward hands – too strong a contact will either cause resistance or loss of activity.

## Combine with other exercises:

With a more advanced horse, use this pattern to set up a working canter pirouette. Ride the pattern in walk, enlarge the circle, strike off to canter, and then immediately ride the same pattern in canter. Linking the two exercises together in this fashion can help the horse better understand what you are asking of him in the canter.

# FIRST STEPS TOWARDS FLYING CHANGES

## 81. COUNTER-FLEXION LEG YIELD IN CANTER

### Aims:

- A highly suppling exercise.
- Addresses obedience to the aids.
- This exercise demands true submission to the bit, with resultant suppleness of the jaw and poll.
- To increase the sideways reach of the horse's shoulders.

### How to:

1. In the corner approaching K in right-lead canter, develop counter-flexion.

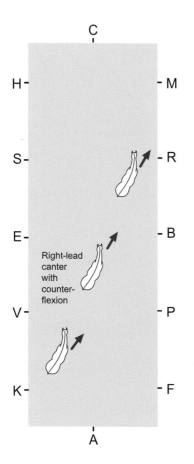

2. At K, whilst maintaining counter-flexion, ask the horse to move sideways on a diagonal line towards the opposite track. Depending on how supple the horse is, you might aim (in the 60m arena) for B, R, or M.

3. Allow the shoulder to lead, and the haunches to trail, to encourage maximum sideways travel.

4. If you arrive at the centre line after X, straighten up, regain true flexion, and ride straight up the centre line. Turn right at C and repeat from M, trying for more sideways displacement.

5. If you cross the centre line well ahead of X, continue to the opposite track where you have two options: regain right flexion and stay in counter-canter, or ride a flying change.

### Common faults:

- *The horse changes lead or becomes disunited.* While you change the horse's flexion for this exercise, do not change your leg or seat position – continue aiding for right-lead canter.

- *The horse does not travel much sideways.* Yield the right rein more extremely to allow the right shoulder to fall towards the right. While this might put the horse out of balance, that very loss of balance will cause the right shoulder to open and take a bigger sideways step.

### Combine with other exercises:

For some horses, this can be a good set-up to teach the flying change. At the end of the diagonal approaching M is a good place to ask – with the horse slightly out of balance in the right-lead canter, and a left flexion in place, the new inside hind can be encouraged to jump forward into left-lead canter. The change may be crooked, but in the early days encouraging the horse to make the change however it happens is the first step.

# 82. SIMPLE CHANGES AROUND THE ARENA

Canter.

## Aims:

- To test out a horse's readiness to start learning flying changes. Once this can be done with ease, the horse is ready to begin changes, but not before.

## How to:

1. Ride around the track in canter.
2. On the long side, make a simple change to the outside lead.
3. Ride around the corner onto the short side in counter canter.
4. Making a simple change at either A or C.
5. Repeat all around the arena, until you can make simple changes both to counter-canter, and to true canter, anywhere you choose around the perimeter of the arena.
6. In a 40m arena aim for at least one simple change on the long side, with one on the short side.
7. In a 60m arena, you should be able to fit in at least two simple changes on a long side, with one on a short side.

## Common faults:

- *The horse loses balance, or does not take increased weight on the haunches in the direct downward transitions to walk.* Work on the weight carriage in the downward transitions using small circles until they improve (see exercise #56).
- *The horse does not always strike off easily into counter-canter.* This indicates he is not genuinely on your aids, which means that flying changes at this stage will not be possible. Work on walk to canter transitions on a straight line *away* from the track, such as the centre line, until you can get whichever lead you request with no hesitancy or mistakes.
- *There is a loss of straightness during the simple change.* Ask for a bare minimum of position towards the new leading leg to maintain control of the shoulders – this will be critical once you start teaching the flying changes.

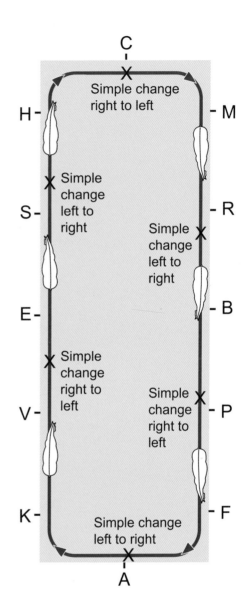

## TOP TIP

Once you can do this exercise with ease, ride a simple change in the position you first intend to ask for the flying change (see exercises #89–#98). Repeat the pattern immediately, and ask for a flying change instead of a simple change.

# FIRST STEPS TOWARDS CANTER PIROUETTES

## 83. REPEATED CANTER COLLECTIONS OVER THE CENTRE LINE

### Aims:

- To use repetition to encourage the horse to make more effort to collect with a minimum of aiding from the rider.
- To prepare for canter pirouettes.

### How to:

1. In collected canter ride a 20m circle in the centre of the school.
2. As you approach the centre line, collect the horse by increasing your core tone, using a smaller seat action, and employing the smallest half-halts on the reins that you can, and still effectively collect. Keep using a quick, but not strong, leg aid.
3. Bring the horse as near to cantering on the spot as you can while you cross the centre line.
4. After three or four steps of ultra-collection, ride forward again to a normal collected canter.
5. Repeat over the following centre line.
6. Keep repeating, until the horse starts to anticipate the collection and you are able to achieve it with less use of rein aids.
7. Once the collections on the circle are easy, try them across the diagonal over X, using the same aids, and then ride forward again. Repeat in both directions – this is one of the positions for pirouettes in tests. Use this to teach the horse to wait for your turning aids, and not to take over.

### Common faults:

- *There is not enough collection.* Once or twice, use more half-halts and hold your seat really still. Imagine your horse cantering on the spot. Provided the horse is strong enough and responsive enough to your aids, it may just take

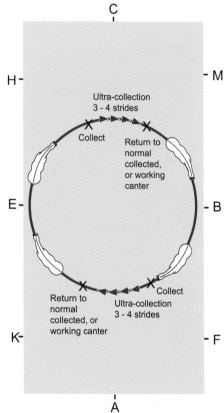

for the rider to dare to ask for more.

- *You lose the canter.* Use lots of quick leg aids, and if necessary, back these up with small taps with the schooling stick – this might be on the flank, or some horses respond better if you touch them on the top of the croup.

### Combine with other exercises:

Once collection becomes easier, instead of riding forward again, ride a few steps of working canter pirouette before going forward again.

# 84. ALTERNATING SHOULDER-FORE AND HAUNCHES-IN, ON THE CIRCLE

Canter.

## Aims:

- To re-confirm the rider's controls of the shoulders and the haunches.
- To increase collection.
- A preparatory exercise for canter pirouette.

## How to:

1. Ride a 20m circle in canter.
2. Move the shoulders *slightly* in, to create shoulder-fore position.
3. Whilst riding around the circle in this position, focus on the feeling of the inside hind stepping under your inside seat bone and carrying you.
4. Do not allow the horse to rush off the hind leg, or conversely, become too slow and lose activity. Ask for energy with a rhythmic use of your inside leg.
5. When you feel you have a good balance, bring the horse's haunches in, until he is in canter travers position. Keep your weight quite central in the saddle as you do this – too much weight to the inside will pull him down onto his inside shoulder, whereas in this position, you now want him to carry more weight on his *outside* hind.
6. You should feel more collection develop. When the horse starts to struggle with the new demand, or when you feel you have what you want in terms of collection, move his shoulders in, and return to shoulder-fore.
7. Repeat.

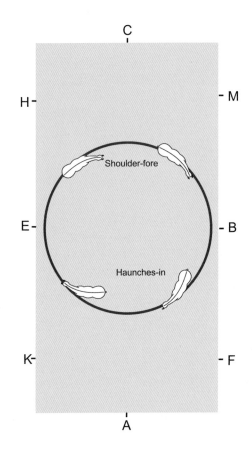

## Common faults:

- *The size and/or shape of the circle deteriorates.* Check the shape of the figure every half-circle and recover it if necessary. Each deviation points to an avoidance of weight carriage by the hind legs.
- *You struggle to turn the shoulders.* Instead of pressing your outside rein steadily against the neck to turn, make repeated press and release, press and release. Horses will sometimes lean against the rein as an evasion – these repetitive aids reduce his ability to lean.

## Combine with other exercises:

Following a few repetitions, when you arrive at the track in shoulder-fore, go straight ahead large around the arena, and ride medium canter, keeping the shoulder-fore position. This both refreshes the canter and utilises the extra weight carriage gained on the circle to improve the quality of the medium strides.

# 85. WORKING PIROUETTE FROM A SPIRAL

## Aims:

- To use the inward spiral (*see* exercise #17) as preparation for the working pirouette by confirming your control of the outside of the horse's body, and the outward spiral as a reward, by reducing the pressure to collect, and by changing the weight carriage from the outside hind (in pirouette) to the inside hind in the leg yield.

## How to:

1. In collected canter, ride an inward spiral from a 20m circle to a 10m circle.
2. On the 10m circle, displace the hindquarters inward to produce haunches in around the small circle – this is a working canter pirouette.
3. *Do not* overload your weight to the inside of the saddle – this will pull the horse onto the inside shoulder. You want him to carry your combined weight on his outside hind, so sit centrally to facilitate this.
4. Once you feel his hindquarters lower, stay on the small circle for just two or three more steps before unwinding the spiral in a gentle outward leg yield.

## Common faults:

- *There is a loss of impulsion, or a loss of quality (jump) in the canter steps.* Use quick leg aids during the working pirouette to chivvy the hind legs to maintain speed and jump. Once you have completed the outward spiral, go immediately forward to medium canter on the 20m circle, before collecting and repeating.
- *The horse loses balance on the working pirouette and spins around, or takes control of the pattern.* Ride haunches-in/working pirouette on a larger circle (say, 15m), and ride out of it as soon as you feel a loss of control. With some horses you might

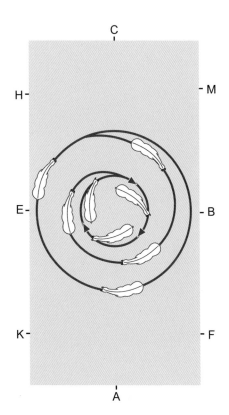

even need to ride out in medium canter to re-establish forwardness. Also, in the pirouette steps try sitting towards the *outside* of the saddle to improve the balance.

## TOP TIP

If the horse becomes anxious, ride just a few steps of working pirouette before enlarging the spiral. Frequent short repetitions will build the horse's confidence that there is an 'escape route' from this challenging exercise.

# WARM-DOWN

## 86. WARM DOWN USING SMALL CIRCLE FIGURES OF EIGHT

**Walk or rising trot.**

### Aims:

- Warming-down is as important as warming-up at the start of an exercise session, so that the horse finishes work with his heart and breathing rates, and his body temperature, back down to resting levels.
- It is also essential for his muscles and mind to be fully relaxed, so that his last memory of a work session is one of comfort, leading to a positive attitude towards work.
- This simple exercise also increases the horse's suppleness by asking for maximum stretch when his body is at its warmest and hence, most pliable.

### How to:

1. In rising trot (or walk) put your horse into a stretched frame, with his poll below his withers and his nose *slightly* in front of the vertical.
2. Choose a size of circle – anything between 20m (novice horses) and 10m (advanced trained horses) – such that he is capable of performing both the circle and the change of direction with fair balance.
3. Starting in the centre of the school at X, ride figure of eights keeping this frame, and ask for more bend (even through the neck) than you would normally expect to achieve.
4. Repeat several times, until the bend feels quite equal in both directions, and the change of bend through the change of direction is accomplished smoothly.

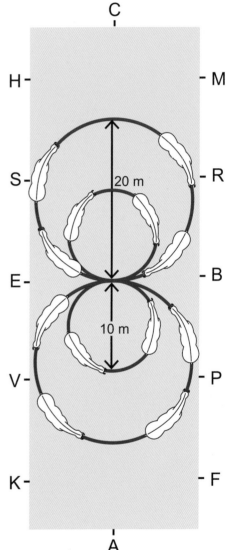

### Common faults:

- *The horse falls in or out on the circles.* Review corrections described in exercise #1.
- *He struggles with maintaining balance during the change of direction.* Review corrections described in exercise #6.

### TOP TIP

If the horse is markedly stiffer in one direction, ride a greater number of circles on that rein, rather than changing direction every time you arrive at X.

# ADVANCED EXERCISES

# EXERCISES TO FURTHER DEVELOP ENGAGEMENT

## 87. PROGRESSIVE SUPPLING CIRCLES

Walk, trot and canter.

### Aims:

- To increase suppleness by gradually increasing demand.
- To check for simultaneous control of shoulders and haunches.
- To use the engaging effect of increasingly smaller circles to develop a greater degree of collection.

### How to:

1. Ride a 10m circle at the first letter of the long side (short arena) or second letter in the long arena.
2. At the next letter, ride an 8m circle.
3. At the next letter, ride a 6m circle
4. If one of the sizes is a struggle, repeat at that size rather than asking for smaller at the next marker.
5. During each circle, monitor your control of the outside shoulder and haunches – this exercise demands precision.

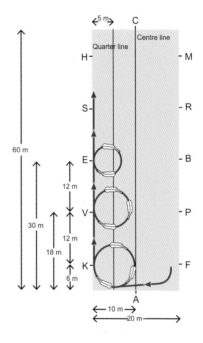

### Common faults:

- *Losing outside shoulder/neck bend only.* Keep the outside rein short enough, and press it inwards and forwards against his neck.
- *Losing quarters.* Check your outside leg position. If the horse pushes out into your outside leg, apply it more strongly and/or further back. Create a slight feeling of haunches-in at the start of the circle, and keep that feeling as you turn the shoulders.
- *Difficulty controlling the size of the circles and/or alignment of the horse's body.* Check and correct both of the above.
- *Horse leans to the inside.* This indicates lack of suppleness in the body. Use your lower inside leg

to push his ribcage to the outside, and your upper inside leg to keep him upright.

- *Rider leans to the inside.* Stretch up through your inside waist and hip – leaning to the inside puts your weight onto your *outside* seat bone, dragging your horse towards the outside of the circle.

### Combine with other exercises:

Use this exercise before riding lateral movements such as shoulder-in, haunches-in, or half-pass. It will give you a more supple and engaged horse prior to the lateral work, along with more precise control of his body bend.

### TOP TIP

Focus on keeping the same rhythm and energy throughout – this will enable you to benefit from the engaging effect of the correctly executed exercise.

# 88. HALF-STEPS ON THE SQUARE

Trot.

## Aims:

- To develop the habit of collection in corners in trot.
- Every corner should be used as an opportunity to gain engagement, and to increase balance and collection. Well-ridden half-steps close the hind legs under the horse's body to achieve this.
- To build the horse's strength and weight carrying capacity.

## How to:

1. Ride a 20m square (*see* exercise #22) in the 60m arena on the right rein, by turning right at E, right at B, right just after P, and right again just before V.
2. About 5m before E, collect the trot to half-steps.
3. At E, return to collected trot and ride around the turn.
4. Ride a normal corner at B, and repeat the half-steps before the next turn off the track.
5. Initially, ride the half-steps on approach to every other turn, simply riding around the intervening turns in trot.
6. Once the horse's strength and reactions improve, ride half-steps on the approach to every turn.

## Common faults:

- *There is a loss of energy in the half-steps.* This may be due either to a lack of response to your aiding, or to a lack of strength. If the former, use stronger, quick leg aids once or twice until he becomes more active. For the latter, ride the half-steps only on every other turn, and at first for fewer steps, until he becomes stronger.
- *The horse loses balance or alignment through the turns.* Take care not to ride too strongly forward as you come out of the half-steps – you may simply be pushing him out of balance.

## Combine with other exercises:

Sometimes ride half-steps as you approach the corners of the arena, to confirm the habit for both horse and rider of increasing engagement around the corners. This would be particularly appropriate when the corner is to be followed by an extended trot.

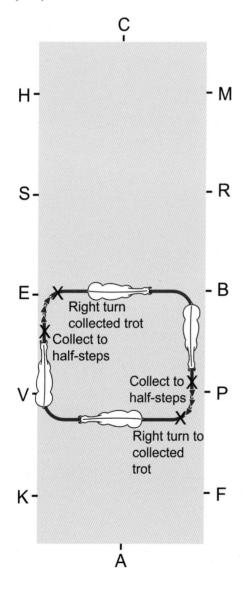

# PATTERNS TO TEACH FLYING CHANGES

## 89. HALF-CIRCLE, RETURN AT OBLIQUE ANGLE TO FLYING CHANGE

### Aims:

- This is one of the first patterns to attempt when teaching the horse flying changes. By returning to the track at an oblique angle, it discourages the horse from trying to run forward when you ask for the change.
- It is most effective when you have either a wall, or a substantial fence, around the arena.

### How to:

1. In the 40m arena, make a half canter circle of around 12m–15m diameter, starting just after the half marker.
2. Ride a diagonal line back towards the track (*see* #10), aiming to arrive a metre or two before the quarter marker.

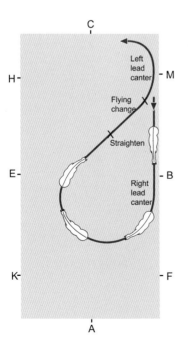

3. Straighten the horse, including the neck. Do not change bend.
4. As you straighten, use the outside leg to activate the outside hind leg ready to make the jump through to the new lead.
5. In the last couple of strides before arriving at the track, ask for the change to the new lead.

### Common faults:

- *The horse runs onto his outside shoulder.* Keep the outside rein firmly against his shoulder as you approach the change, and use more outside leg right up until the moment of asking for the change.
- *The horse ignores your aid and does not change leads.* Try tapping him lightly with the whip on the outside hind leg for a stride or two *before* asking for the change.
- *The change is late behind.* Use the same preparation as immediately above – you need the hind leg active and ready to jump. If he bucks a little behind during this preparation, do not discourage it – it is more likely he will change if his hind leg is already springing his hindquarters upwards!
- *The change is late in front.* This indicates the horse's balance is too much on his shoulders. Improve engagement and collection of the canter before trying again.

### TOP TIP

If the horse does not change cleanly at first, still praise him, and then repeat with better preparation. To begin with, you are simply introducing the concept of changing leads – correctness and quality come later, with confidence.

# 90. CANTER HALF-PASS TO FLYING CHANGE

## Aims:

- Half-pass is an excellent set up for a flying change. The half-pass requires collection and secures the connection from leg to hand whilst encouraging the horse to take more weight on the inside hind leg – all of which make the change easier to produce.
- The horse is also focused on the outside leg (the dominant leg aid) in the half-pass, so when the leg positions are changed, it will be very clear you are asking for the opposite lead.

## How to:

1. From the centre line, ride canter half-pass, aiming to arrive at the track around three strides before the quarter marker.
2. *Straighten* the horse and ride positively forward on the track for a couple of steps, and then ask for a flying change.
3. Use the short side to re-balance the horse and calm any excitement associated with the flying change.
4. Either circle, or ride large, around the arena until the horse is relaxed before repeating the pattern in the other direction.

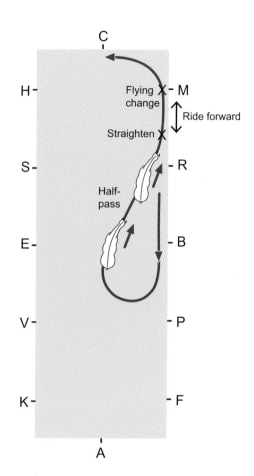

## Common faults:

- *The horse does not change the lead.* Repeat, but as you straighten up, tap the horse with the whip behind your outside leg. This is the hind leg that must make the biggest jump through to the new lead, so activate it before asking for the change.
- *The change is late behind.* Same correction as above.
- *The change is late in front.* See corrections in exercise #89.
- *The horse becomes nervous and rushes forwards after the change.* Return to walk as soon as you can, and encourage him to relax and stretch in order to pump the adrenaline out of his system before continuing.
- *The horse anticipates and makes the change before you ask for it.* Ride the half-pass *without* a change several times before asking for it again.

### TOP TIP

Make sure to truly straighten from the half-pass before asking for the change. You may even find it helpful to position him shoulder-fore towards the new lead *before* asking for the change.

# 91. FLYING CHANGES ON THE SHORT DIAGONALS

20m × 60m arena.

## Aims:

- This pattern takes advantage of the collecting effect of the preparatory short turn, and at the same time, the effect of the fence ahead to discourage the horse from running forwards.

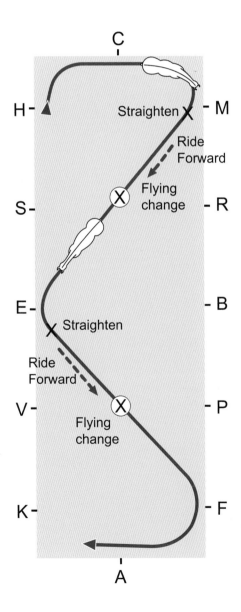

## How to:

1. On the right rein, collect through the short side HCM.
2. Use a fairly deep corner between C and M to increase engagement.
3. Turn onto the short diagonal, heading towards E.
4. Straighten fully and ride the canter a little more forward for three steps.
5. Ask for the flying change to the left lead as you cross the centre line.
6. Re-balance and collect the canter following the change, and remain straight until you arrive at E.

Then either:

1. Use the turn at E in the same manner as you used the corner before M for preparation, and then turn across the next short diagonal from E to F, with a flying change to the right lead over the centre line.
2. Continue down the long side from E to K, and repeat in the opposite direction from F towards E.

## Common faults:

- *The change does not happen as required.* See exercise #89 for a comprehensive set of corrections.
- *The horse is unbalanced after the change.* Focus on using the turn at E to help re-balance, and then either ride down the long side (option #2 above), or put a 10m circle at E to assist the recovery of balance and engagement before taking option #1 above.

### TOP TIP

Try placing 10m circles into this pattern before and after the short diagonals, to gain more engagement and balance in preparation for the changes.

# 92. TWO HALF-CIRCLES WITH FLYING CHANGE

## Aims:

- Another basic pattern for introducing the horse to flying changes, particularly if he tends to panic and run forward.

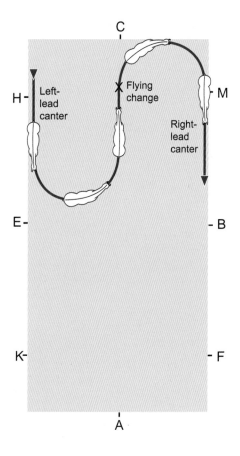

## How to:

1. In left-lead canter, a few metres after H, ride a 10m half-circle onto the centre line, facing C.

2. For a few repetitions, ride a simple change so that you are turning away to the right at C, in right-lead canter.

3. Positioning is critical for this exercise to be effective: the horse should be heading directly into the fence or wall at C to discourage running forward, which would allow him to ignore the change aid.

4. Once the simple change is calmly performed, ride the same pattern but substitute the aids for the flying change instead of riding simple change.

## Common faults:

- *The horse anticipates the simple change and tries to walk.* Ride the approaching canter more positively forward.

- *The horse throws his balance onto the new inside shoulder.* Make sure that *you* are not shifting your weight too hard or suddenly into the new direction. Keep the old outside rein more firmly against the shoulder as you ask for the change.

### TOP TIP

Unless the horse finds learning flying changes easy, establish the change in just one direction first. Attempting to teach both ways in the same session can often lead to confidence issues, so be patient and establish one at a time.

# 93. CANTER LEG YIELD INTO FLYING CHANGE

## Aims:

- Another example of how to introduce the horse to flying changes.
- The leg yield activates the old outside hind ready to make the jump through to the new lead.

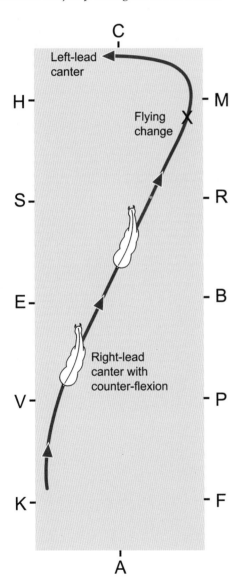

- The horse is already in the new bend, and with his weight on the new outside shoulder, which helps prevent him from throwing his weight to the inside – one of the most common ways to evade performing the change.

## How to:

1. Review exercise #81.
2. Ride canter leg yield in counter-flexion across the whole arena. Aim to finish the leg yield at the track a few metres before a corner – you will need to estimate where to begin, depending on how easily your horse moves sideways.
3. A stride or two before reaching the track, ask for the flying change.

## Common faults:

- *The flying change is late behind.* This can be a consequence of using this pattern, as it has a tendency to put the body weight more over the shoulders. Monitor the balance as you ride sideways, and try to keep the horse upright. You may need to reduce the amount of counter-flexion you ask for during the leg yield. Use taps with the whip on the old outside/new inside hind leg prior to asking for the change.
- *The horse runs forward when you ask for the change.* Try making the change a few strides later, as you are facing the wall/fence enclosing the corner.

## TOP TIP

This will not give you a straight change. However, it is a good way to explain to the horse what you want him to do with his legs, and then you can work on straightening up the changes once he is more confident about responding to the flying change aids.

# 94. FLYING CHANGE ON THE HALF SCHOOL LINE

## Aims:

- A good preparatory exercise prior to attempting flying changes on a serpentine.
- The short turn helps collect the horse, and teaches the rider how to straighten the horse coming out of a curved line.

## How to:

1. In left-lead canter, turn left at B.
2. Start to straighten *before* completing the turn.
3. Ride directly forward two or three steps, depending on the size of the horse's stride.
4. In the stride before X, ask for the flying change – this gives the horse time to react, and make the change as he passes over X. Keep your eyes fixed on E during the change and ride straight towards the letter.
5. Ride a couple of straight strides before turning right at E.

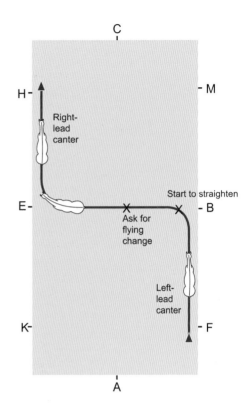

## Common faults:

- For issues with the change itself, *see* exercise #89 for corrections.
- *The horse falls on his left shoulder-in on the first turn, and is not balanced enough to make the change.* Take the time to correct his straightness. For a few times, ride across the arena to E and then turn left, without attempting a change. Come round and re-present him, making sure you have him genuinely connected from left leg to right rein in the turn to keep him upright, and that you are not turning by using the inside rein.
- *The horse falls onto his right shoulder as you make the change, and loses the line towards E.* Keep a more positive contact on your left (new outside) rein

during and after the change, and use a firm inside leg to create the correct connection for the new canter lead and to keep him straight.

## Combine with other exercises:

Once the horse is confident with this pattern, in the 20m x 60m arena, ride the first turn across the P–V line, and then make a second turn from S–R. This becomes a square serpentine with changes across the centre line, preparatory to riding a proper curved serpentine.

# 95. FLYING CHANGES OUT OF THE CIRCLE

### Aims:

- To further develop already established flying changes – do not ride this exercise on a horse that is not yet confident in the changes.
- To check that the flying changes are genuinely on your aids, waiting for your signal, and not done merely by rote in a learned place in the arena.
- This exercise is particularly good for improving the flying changes on the serpentine.

### How to:

1. Canter a 20m circle in the centre of the arena on the inside canter lead.
2. As you approach the centre line each time, change flexion to the outside.
3. Once you have crossed the centre line, change back to true flexion.
4. Once the horse remains calm, supple, balanced and attentive, and *waits* for your aids, ask for a flying change as you cross the centre line and immediately turn away to the new direction.
5. As this circle is positioned in the centre of the arena, in every circle you have two options for where to make the change.

### Common faults:

- *When you change flexion, the horse attempts to make a flying change without waiting for the aid.* This is one of the purposes of this exercise – to make the horse wait and listen – so ensure you are very clear with your leg and seat positions that you intend to remain on the inside canter lead until you are ready to make the change. If an unrequested change does occur, drop immediately to walk and pick up the inside canter lead again.
- *The horse does not respond when you ask for the flying change.* This indicates the horse is not truly on your aids. Next time you ask, exaggerate your aids. If there is still no response, try tapping the outside hind with the whip prior to asking – this is the hind leg that needs to take the bigger step through to make the flying change, and this tapping can make the horse both more attentive, and more active with that specific hind leg.

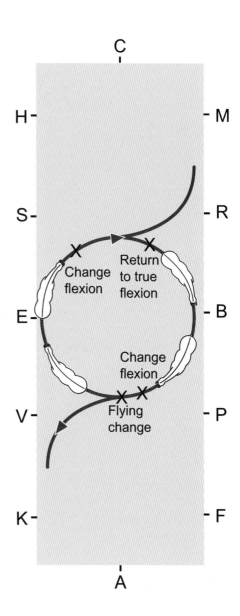

**TOP TIP**

Take care not to throw your weight to the side when you ask for the change – this will unbalance the horse and either prevent the change, or encourage it to be late behind.

# 96. FLYING CHANGES IN AND OUT OF A CIRCLE

## Aims:

- Riding flying changes on a circle is a good technique for increasing forwardness and hence gaining greater expression in the changes.
- It is also a great pattern to use for advanced level freestyle tests.

## How to:

1. In right-lead canter, ride a 20m circle at E.
2. As you approach B, push a little more with your outside leg to prepare for the flying change – this both engages the hind leg that must take the longest step, and straightens the horse.
3. At B, ride a flying change to the outside lead.
4. Ride the next half of the circle in counter-canter. As you approach E, use your outside (which, of course, will be your right leg, even though it is on the inside of the circle) leg to prepare the next change.
5. At E, ride a flying change to the inside.
6. Repeat.
7. When these are easy, ride the changes over the centre lines, where you do not have the support of the wall to assist with straightness and balance.

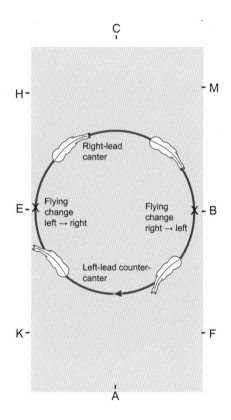

## Common faults:

- *The horse anticipates and does the change before you ask. See* the previous exercise for this correction.
- *The horse does not change at all. See* the previous exercise for this correction.
- *The horse swings in the flying change.* You may have used too strong a leg aid, or the horse has dropped onto his forehand. Check that he stays up in front as you ride the next change, and use a lighter leg aid.

## TOP TIP

Once you can ride a change each way in and out of the circle at E and B, and over the centre lines, try riding changes at all of those points on the same circle, so that you have four changes per circle.

Eventually you should be able to ride counted tempi changes around the perimeter of the circle – always a crowd- (and judge-!) pleaser – in a freestyle test.

# 97. THREE- AND FOUR-LOOP SERPENTINES WITH FLYING CHANGES

Canter.

## Aims:

- To assess the ease of straightening the horse from the serpentine loop on the approach to the change.
- To check out the equality of the changes in the two directions.

## How to:

1. In the 40m arena, begin a three-loop serpentine. In the 60m arena, begin a four-loop serpentine.
2. As you come out of the curve of the first loop, straighten the horse.
3. There will only be a stride or two after completing the loop before you will cross the centre line, so begin your straightening by taking a half-halt on the outside rein *before* you are fully around the loop.
4. In the stride before the centre line, apply the flying change aid.
5. In a three-loop serpentine, you will make one flying change to either direction, and end up on the same lead.
6. In a four-loop serpentine you will make two flying changes in one direction, and one in the other, to end up on the opposite lead from the one in which you began the exercise.

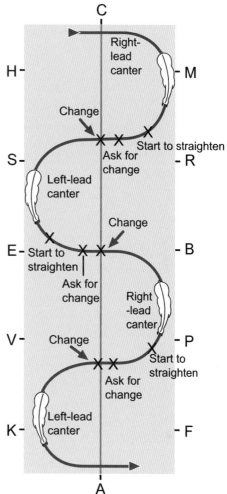

## Common faults:

- *One or more of the flying changes is faulty, or does not happen at all.* Practise making flying changes out of a circle (exercise #95), before returning to the serpentine.
- *The changes happen after the centre line.* You must straighten earlier, and apply the aids within two steps of completing the curve of each loop. This exercise requires precision in the timing, and control of the horse's straightness.
- *As the serpentine progresses, the shape of the figure, and the positioning of the flying changes, becomes increasingly hard to achieve.* This means the canter needs more collection.

### TOP TIP

Initially, ride the loops with minimal, or no, bending. This removes the urgency to straighten the horse before you arrive at the flying change.

# 98. FLYING CHANGES TO THE OUTSIDE LEAD

### Aims:

- This is the first step towards riding tempi changes, and checks that the horse is genuinely making the changes on your aids, and not just because he has learned to do them in particular positions in the school.

### How to:

1. In a regular inside canter lead, ride along the inside track (exercise #20) to ensure straightness.
2. Once the horse is straight and balanced, ask for a flying change to the outside lead, while remaining on the inside track.
3. Continue down the inside track and around the short side in counter-canter.
4. Change rein across the diagonal (use medium canter if you need to increase energy).
5. Repeat on the next long side of the arena.
6. Once this exercise is established, make the flying change to the outside before the half marker, and then change back to the inside lead before reaching the short side (or even on the short side, at either A or C).
7. Initially, when starting tempi changes do not worry about counting strides between the changes, just get the horse confident in changing to both directions on your aids without a pattern to help set them up.

### Common faults:

- *The change to the outside lead does not happen.* Go back a step, and ride some more changes from outside lead to inside lead, making sure the horse is listening to your aids before trying again. If the change still does not happen, counter-flex him and ride a couple of steps of leg yield *away* from the inside track before asking for the change.

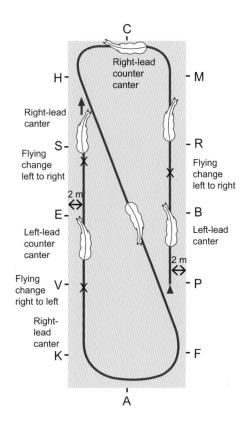

### Combine with other exercises:

Once the horse is confident with this exercise, try making a flying change either way on the diagonal – again, do not count strides between the changes, just get one each way. After this, in the 20m × 60m arena, try three changes, still without counting.

Beyond this, you can start to count four strides between changes, and eventually introduce five flying changes to each diagonal.

# DEVELOPING THE CANTER ZIGZAG

## 99. PREPARATION EXERCISE FOR THE CHANGEOVER IN THE CANTER ZIGZAG

### Aims:

- As the difficulty of the zigzag increases, with multiple changeovers, and eventually, counted strides of half-pass, the necessity for a smooth and easy change of direction involving the flying change becomes essential if the movement is to be performed with ease.
- This exercise teaches horse and rider the positioning required prior to the flying change, and trains the horse to wait for the change aid.

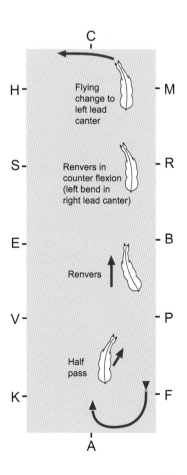

### How to:

1. On the right rein in right-lead canter, turn onto the centre line at A.
2. Half-pass right to the quarter line.
3. Continue straight down the quarter line, but push the horse's hips out to the right, maintaining the right bend for a few steps (renvers position).
4. Change the bend, so that you will be travelling down the quarter line in left bend, with his hips to the right of the line, still in right lead canter.
5. Next, either:
6. Change the lead just before the end of the arena.
7. Or continue around the short side, holding this position and change the lead only when you feel the horse has accepted the requirement to wait for your aid.

### Common faults:

- *The horse changes canter lead without you asking.* The point of this exercise is that he must learn to wait, so immediately he makes a change, ride a transition to walk and go back and start the exercise again.
- *The horse loses balance when you change the bend.* This implies a need for more lateral suppleness, and a return to work on basic suppling exercises.

### Combine with other exercises:

If you feel you can achieve the haunches-out position and change the bend without the horse anticipating, you can make the flying change as soon as you are ready, and go immediately into the new (left, in the above example) half-pass.

# 100. ZIGZAG WITH POLES

**Walk, trot and canter.**
**The following description informs the most difficult of the three, in canter.**

## Aims:

- To give the rider a clear understanding of the distribution of a zigzag.
- The example is for a three-leg zigzag.
- For the five legs of the Grand Prix zigzag, you can replace the poles with a single marker such as a cone, but the principle is the same.

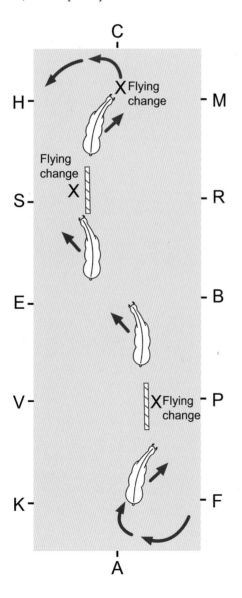

## How to:

1. In the 20m × 60m arena, lay poles on the ground as depicted in the diagram.
2. On the right rein, in right-lead canter, turn onto the centre line at A.
3. Half-pass right keeping the first pole in front of you.
4. Once you have passed the pole, make a change to left lead (*see exercise #99 for the preparatory steps to riding a changeover*), and begin a left half-pass.
5. Keep the second pole in front of you and do the same procedure in reverse.
6. Finish in half-pass right to the centre line.
7. At the centre line, straighten, make a flying change to the left, and turn left at C.

## Common faults:

- *Not half-passing steeply enough to keep the upcoming pole in front of you.* Start the half-pass more promptly from the turn, and make sure to look at the pole as you ride sideways to keep it in front of you.
- *Going too far past the end of the pole.* This will then give you too steep an angle in the next half-pass – keep the changeover as close to the pole as you can.
- *Running out of room on the final half-pass because you do not have a pole to guide you.* You can always add a pole to the side of the centre line if you find this helps your aim.

## TOP TIP

Because of their natural tendency to bend differently on their two sides, horses will often half-pass more sideways in one direction than the other. Always return to basic suppling exercises to improve the equality of the two directions.

# PATTERNS TO DEVELOP CANTER PIROUETTES

## 101. QUARTER CANTER PIROUETTES ON THE SQUARE

**Aims:**

- To develop the skill of moving the shoulders around the haunches, and to keep the balance within those steps.
- To teach the horse to leave the pirouette with energy, and not to get stuck.

**How to:**

1. Ride a 20m square – *see exercise #22*.
2. On alternate corners (leaving the track), collect, bend the horse to the inside, and turn the shoulders around the haunches, using outside leg and rein.
3. Once the horse has achieved a 90-degree turn (usually two steps), ride forward, encouraging an energetic departure from the quarter pirouette.

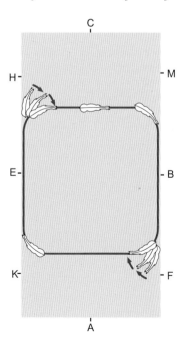

4. At first, ride the intervening corners with a normal degree of collection.
5. Once the exercise feels easy, both coming into, and out of, the pirouette steps, start to ride quarter pirouettes on every corner.
6. Once that is easy, reduce the size of the square down to 10m.

**Common faults:**

- *The horse swings his hindquarters out.* Review his response to your displacing leg aid.
- *You struggle to turn the shoulders faster than the haunches.* Find more collection before asking. Use *less* outside leg, and more outside rein, pushing it inwards towards the crest and forward enough not to restrict movement.
- *The horse falls in and overturns.* Check that your weight is central in the saddle, and apply your inside leg as soon as you have achieved one step, to ride forward out of the turn sooner.
- *The horse does not move immediately forward following the quarter-pirouette.* Once or twice, as you leave a pirouette, abandon your rein contact and use sudden strong leg aids to startle the horse into running forward. The horse must understand that the 'door' is always open in front of him – he should never feel trapped by the exercise.

**Combine with other exercises:**

Ride a few canter squares with quarter-pirouettes, and then go forward to medium canter around the arena. Collect and repeat the square. Interspersing collected work with medium gaits refreshes the canter and teaches the horse to think forward coming out of pirouettes.

# 102. SERPENTINE WITH CANTER WORKING HALF-PIROUETTES

## Aims:

- To enable frequent repetition, during the learning phase, of canter half-pirouettes without changing direction.

## How to:

1. In canter right, begin a four-loop serpentine from A.
2. At the centre line, collect the canter towards pirouette canter.
3. At the quarter line, perform a working canter half-pirouette right.
4. Proceed onto the second serpentine loop and repeat each time you cross the centre line during the serpentine.

## Common faults:

- *Over-collecting the canter.* This can cause a loss of impulsion and jump in the canter, such that the half-pirouette becomes a struggle. Only collect as much as the horse is able to do, and still maintain canter quality. Go back and work on exercises to collect the canter: *see exercise #83.*
- *Over-turning the half-pirouette.* If you do not end up coming out on the correct line, next time, look up and look for your line as you turn, and start to ride forward out of the half-pirouette *before* the final stride.
- *The horse spins round.* Ride the half-pirouette larger, using your inside leg to maintain a more forward-travelling canter.

## Combine with other exercises:

Adapt this pattern by riding one half-pirouette right between loops one and two, then continue a regular serpentine with a flying change over X, followed by a half-pirouette left between loops three and four. This is another pleasing pattern to include in a freestyle test.

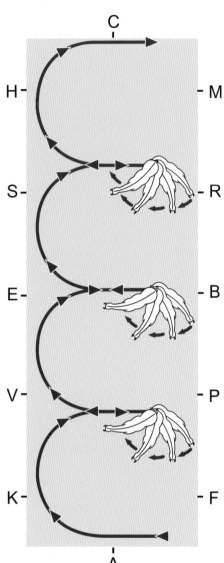

## TOP TIP

Once the horse performs two fairly good half-pirouettes in succession, end the exercise in that direction. Repeating beyond that point may tire his muscles too much.

# 103. WALK PIROUETTE INTO CANTER PIROUETTE

## Aims:

- To use the walk pirouette to engage the hindquarters immediately before the canter pirouette.
- Horses will often associate the idea of the pirouette performed in walk and transfer this to the canter provided there is a minimal gap between the two movements, making this another method of teaching the horse what you want him to do in a pirouette.

## How to:

1. Near to the centre line, perform a full (360-degree) walk pirouette to the right.
2. At the end of the pirouette, make a transition to right-lead canter (review exercise #59).
3. Within two steps, ask for a canter pirouette and go round as far as the horse can manage without struggling.
4. Ride out of the pirouette and either go forward to medium canter (if the canter has lost impulsion), or make a transition to walk.
5. Repeat.
6. If the horse becomes agitated in the walk, drop the reins and change rein a few times at free walk until he relaxes before picking up the contact to repeat.

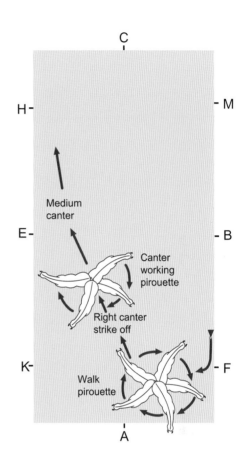

## Common faults:

- *There is a delay when you ask for the canter strike off.* Work on the promptness of reaction to the canter alone, without going into the canter pirouette. The walk pirouette lowers the horse's croup, increasing the demand for strength within the transition. If this step is a struggle, it suggests the horse is not yet strong enough to perform a canter pirouette.
- *The horse runs through the bridle when you ask for the canter pirouette.* For a couple of times, ride walk pirouette, transition to canter, followed by transition to walk. This will keep him collected in the canter and teach him to wait.

## TOP TIP

As with other exercises in extreme collection, it is always good practice to go forward to a medium as soon as you complete the pattern, both to recover any impulsion lost by the extra physical demand, and as confirmation to the horse that when he performs an exercise well, the rider will reward him by removing the pressure of the demand.

# 104. THE 'V' SHAPE

### Aims:

- To reassure the horse that tends to feel 'stuck' in pirouettes, and potentially panic. This might happen because the horse loses balance, over-sits, tries to overturn, or because of anxiety about the degree of collection.
- To put the horse in front of your inside leg, without undue pressure on hindquarters that are still developing the strength required for pirouettes.
- Teaches the horse to think forward *out* of pirouettes.
- For the nervous horse, and the lazy horse, it develops confidence by showing them that there is an 'escape route' from pirouette.

### How to:

1. In left-lead canter, start on the diagonal from F–H.
2. At X, ride two steps of a pirouette.
3. Go out of the pirouette steps on the line towards K as fast as you can go! Do not worry about the outline as you go – slack reins will ensure the enthusiasm of departure and give confidence to the nervous horse.
4. Re-establish your rein contact as you approach K.
5. Collect on the short side and repeat from F.

### Common faults:

- *The horse overturns, and ends up facing A.* Ride forward out of the pirouette sooner. Use more inside leg to keep the horse travelling more forward with less turning, to end up on the correct line out. Also check that you do not have too much weight to the inside – sit centrally in the saddle rather than weighting the inside seat bone.
- *There is a loss of impulsion in the pirouette steps.* You are only asking for two steps, so you can afford to be more demanding that he keeps the energy – use more inside leg and driving (scooping) seat.

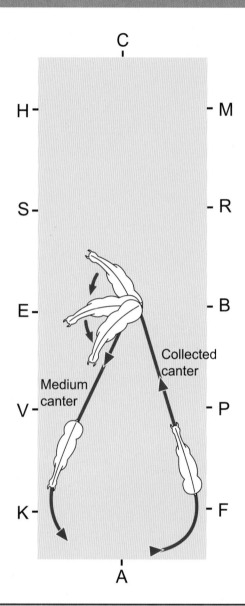

**TOP TIP**

In pirouette, sit either in the centre of the saddle, or even with slightly more weight in your *outside* seat bone to prevent pulling him down onto his inside shoulder, which causes spinning or overturning.

# 105. CANTER HALF-PASS TO WORKING PIROUETTE

### Aims:

- To develop canter pirouettes with maintenance of the positioning throughout the exercise.
- Confirm the ability to move the shoulders and haunches independently.

### How to:

1. Turn onto the quarter line in right-lead canter.
2. Half-pass right to the opposite quarter line.
3. Immediately ride a working canter pirouette (haunches-in around a small half-circle) right.
4. Go out of the pirouette directly into right canter half-pass.
5. At the next quarter line, repeat.
6. The aim is to maintain the right bend and positioning throughout the exercise, but move the shoulders at different speeds relative to the haunches, depending on which part of the exercise is being ridden.

### Common faults:

- *There is a loss of impulsion in the working pirouette.* Make the working pirouette larger, but maintain the haunches in aspect around the half-circle.
- *The shoulders lead too much in half-pass.* Use more half-halts on the outside rein to slow the shoulders and displace the haunches more sideways relative to the shoulders.
- *The horse drops onto the shoulders during the half-pass.* If the balance is a struggle, go back to working on strengthening and collecting exercises. Do not repeat the pattern too many times, or you may tire the horse's carrying (haunch) muscles.

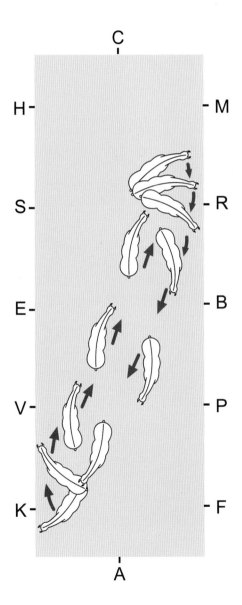

### TOP TIP

As the exercise becomes easier, ride a step or two straight on each quarter line both out of and into the half-pass, and reduce the size of the half-circle until it becomes a genuine pirouette.

# 106. CANTER HALF-PIROUETTE ON THE QUARTER LINE

## Aims:

- To encourage the horse to take more weight onto the hind legs.
- To limit the size of the half-pirouette.

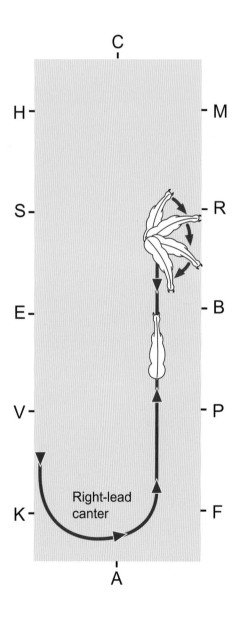

C

H -        - M

S -        - R

E -        - B

V -        - P

Right-lead canter

K -        - F

A

## How to:

1. In right-lead *counter*-canter, ride along the quarter line (five metres inside the track).
2. Once balance and straightness are established, collect the canter.
3. Make a half-pirouette to the right. You will be turning towards the track, using the fence to limit how large the pirouette can be.
4. Proceed along the three-quarter line, now in true canter.

## Common faults:

- *Seeing the fence in front of him, the horse drops the left shoulder and spins away to the left, refusing to make the pirouette turn.* Initially, ride a line seven or eight metres away from the track, until the horse does not feel trapped by the exercise, and then on repetition, gradually move the line closer to the track again.
- *The horse loses impulsion or breaks to trot.* Make sure your collection has plenty of energy before turning the pirouette. If this is still a struggle, follow the above advice to modify the pattern to make it slightly easier in the short term.

## Combine with other exercises:

Upon leaving the pirouette, ride forward to medium canter. Teaching the horse to leave pirouettes with enthusiasm is good practice before you attempt to ride them in competition.

# PART 2

# TRAINING STRATEGIES

# PLAN YOUR SCHOOLING SESSIONS

Many riders believe schooling to be boring, both for themselves and their horses. If you start a schooling session with no goal and no plan, that is quite likely to be the outcome. This section of the book is designed to offer some idea of goals to aim at, and sequences of patterns to achieve those physical goals while engaging both the rider's and the horse's brains for a more satisfying experience.

At the same time, it is essential to take a flexible approach, because horses are not machines. Like us, they have good days and bad days, and that can mean that any pre-made plans might have to be changed 'on the hoof'. Take a moment during your warm-up to assess how your horse feels that day, and learn to respond appropriately, rather than simply riding the patterns you have pre-chosen for the day. Use the Scales of Training (discussed in the introduction of this book) as your template, and this will give you a starting point for every schooling session.

As your experience increases you will find this easier, and schooling will become a rewarding experience, instead of feeling like a chore.

---

## THE PURPOSE OF TRAINING

Never be afraid to let your schooling get messy. The purpose of training is to *expose* weaknesses and work through the issues to fix them – not to cover them up. Disguising a problem does not make it go away, it means that at a later date you will have to backtrack and waste time sorting out an issue that could, and should, have been addressed when it first became apparent.

---

## GOAL SETTING

By setting goals you will give your schooling more than just a vague purpose.

Goals come in three categories:
1. Short term.
2. Mid-term.
3. Long term.

Schooling examples of goals would be:
1. Short term – to improve the horse's bend on his stiffer side.
2. Mid-term – to compete in a Preliminary dressage test.
3. Long term – to achieve Medium training level.

Or for a more established horse:
1. Short term – to improve the bend in half-pass.
2. Mid-term – to learn flying changes.
3. Long term – to compete in Advanced tests.

Horses being horses, it is also important to realise that these goals need to be flexible to accommodate all the many things that can go wrong, or derail plans. If, for example, your goal is to compete in a particular championship, but your horse picks up an injury that means this is no longer possible, rather than becoming despondent, respond by revising your goal to entering the same show the following year, but at a higher level. Once your horse is recovered, you can use the intervening time to progress him further up the competition ladder.

Re-appraising your goals every so often is good practice, taking into account the timeframe of your recent progress. Unrealistic goals, particularly short-term, can be dispiriting. To maintain enthusiasm and the positive mental attitude that will keep you calmly focused and feeling satisfied, you need to know that you *can* achieve the goals you have set yourself.

## BASIC STRUCTURE OF A TRAINING SESSION

There is no question that the novice horse – whether a young horse, or simply an inexperienced horse of any age – is more limited in the patterns that can be employed, so the more variety of simple patterns in your repertoire, the more interest you can add to each schooling session.

An average schooling session will last approximately 40–45 minutes, split into three phases:
1. Warm-up (10–15 minutes).

2. Work (25–30 minutes), **to include at least one short rest break**, possibly more.

3. Warm-down (5–10 minutes).

Only extremely fit horses should be worked for longer than this. Exhausting the horse's muscles will not be productive in terms of either physical or mental education. If the horse 'needs' to be worked longer before it becomes 'sensible', then either the general management needs reassessing, or the approach to a specific type of temperament needs adjustment – see below.

For a younger horse, 20–30 minutes in total is plenty, with the work section shortened down to 10–15 minutes.

It is also important to be flexible in terms of time. If the horse does something particularly well, such as learning a new movement or aid, or makes a good effort in something he finds hard, such as bending well on his stiffer side, the rider/trainer should recognise this by ending work immediately, no matter how short the session ends up being. The horse should either be returned to the field or stable, or taken for a hack in place of warming down.

In fact, both warm-up and warm-down can be replaced by hacking with horses at any stage in their training.

Lungeing can also be used as part of the warm-up for horses that are either recently backed, or need to use up a little excess energy before the rider mounts, but should not extend the entire session by more than a few minutes.

## IF YOU ARE SHORT OF TIME

If you are short of time, *do not* try to compress an entire schooling session into a shorter time frame – it will not work! Instead, ride a good warm-up, and if that is all there is time for, finish the session there. Trying to work the horse without warming-up may cause physical damage, and sour the horse's attitude to work as a result.

# GENERAL ADVICE FOR SCHOOLING SESSIONS:

- Quality is better than quantity – if the horse does something particularly well, consider ending the schooling session and possibly cool down by going for a hack.

- Alternate demanding work with periods of stretching, which can be done in any gait – simply allowing the horse to stretch refreshes the muscles before going back to work again.

- If the horse struggles with something, go back to an earlier exercise to re-confirm his understanding before returning to the more difficult exercise. *See* an example below, for half-pass.

- If the horse's energy level is reduced by the demands of an exercise, refresh it by going forward once or twice in medium trot or canter before returning to the harder exercise.

- Finishing out a session with either medium, or stretchy work helps to leave the horse with a memory of feeling good from a work out, and not in pain of overused muscles.

- Depending on the horse's temperament type (*see* below) it can be a good strategy to end the work session (before warming-down) with medium trot or canter, to end on a positive forward note, especially if the session has concentrated on engagement or collection.

- Make sure to warm-down thoroughly at the end of the session by stretching and slowing the gait. The goal is to take the horse back to the stable with muscles that feel comfortable and pliable, so that his last memory of the schooling session is one of feeling good about his body.

# TACTICS FOR SCHOOLING HORSES OF DIFFERENT TEMPERAMENTS

To train horses successfully one must take into account that horses have a variety of differing temperaments, and sessions should be designed to use considered strategies proven to work for each type of horse. Horses are individuals, and what works for one will not necessarily work for another.

There are general tactics for different temperaments that should underlie schooling sessions, particularly with regard to the warm-up. Sometimes a horse might have a combination of the following traits, and you may need, as ever, to be flexible in your approach to discover what works best on any given day.

## Energetic, fizzy horses

Ride a lot of circle patterns, especially spirals. This type of horse is best kept on the turn, so that they constantly see the same area of the arena in front of them. Seeing an open vista before them, as they do when you ride large around the arena, is an invitation to gain speed and excitement, so avoid long straight lines, at least until the horse is truly on your aids and fully in work mode.

Using circles also absorbs extra energy, simply by engaging the inside hind more under the body as a result of the constant bend in the horse's frame. This allows the rider better control of speed and energy without having to resort to restraining aids, which might frustrate both horse and rider.

Remain with a pattern until the horse settles, so make changes of rein infrequently, and when you do, use curved patterns, such as two connected half-circles (#6 or #7), or serpentines with even numbers of loops (#12).

As the horse starts to listen more to the aids, begin to ride short stretches of straight lines to interconnect the circles, always turning away onto a circle if either the speed, or tension, increases.

Transitions will be effective for some horses of this type, making them slow down and think. With others, transitions may be too exciting, so you need to discover what works best for the individual.

With the advanced horse there is also the option to use plenty of lateral work for the same reason as the circles – by engaging one hind leg at a time it is easier to maintain control of the excess power produced by this type of horse without causing frustration.

## Lazy, unmotivated horses

The converse of the above is appropriate for this type of horse. Avoid much in the way of circles until the horse is motivated to work. Ride more open, straight lines, so that he always has a fresh view in front of him. Ride large around the arena, and use such patterns as shallow loops (#8) quarter lines and inside tracks (#20), centre lines (#11), and long line changes of rein (#4, #5 & #10).

Include the occasional large circle (#1 and #6), to help his suppleness, but only one, or at most two, before going large again. Avoid smaller circles. Circles are harder work than straight lines because of the extra engagement they demand, and so tend to add to a lack of motivation.

Include plenty of changes of gait. Transitions are useful to exercise the hind legs, wake up muscles, and hone responses, and also add interest to the work.

With most horses, you can also include easy leg yield patterns (see #33 and #39), which assist with both suppleness and engagement, while remaining with the open pattern strategy to keep the horse's view of the arena fresh.

## Nervous and easily distracted horses

Similar to the energetic horse, there is an added component to be considered with this type of temperament. Nervousness and lack of attention point directly to horses that lack balance. In the wild, the horse that is unbalanced is the one that is most likely to fall over and get eaten! As a consequence, at an instinctive level, being unbalanced is anxiety-making for any horse.

This type of horse should also be kept focused inward on circles and smaller patterns, while remaining within his physical capabilities. Anything that puts him out of balance will add to his stress levels. This may come out in a tendency to gain speed, which goes right back to the natural flight response. Attempting to control this type of horse with your aids will only add to the problem.

Instead, use the above suggestions for the fizzy horse, but also make use of keeping him close to the track – which provides psychological security – as much as you can. So, position your circles in corners, where they are enclosed by two sides of the track, make downward transitions as you face the fence so the 'backing off' effect of a fence in front of the horse means that you can use minimal aiding, and keep everything as slow as you can (to help him feel balanced) without frustrating him.

If he is capable, lateral work performed on a circle is an excellent tactic for this type of horse because it keeps him in one location, and at the same time engages him which improves his balance. See exercises #51 and #58. Also, leg yield along the wall (#36), and short-distance lateral work on the straight line, combined with circles: #48 & #55.

## Smart horses

These are often the trickiest, because in the earlier stages of training, their bodies are not physically capable of doing too much in terms of either length of work session, or difficulty of movement. Intelligent horses will often look for mischief, because their brain is way ahead of what their body can do, and with the goal of training a horse to have a long and sound life, it is important not to give in and teach the horse more demanding movements at too early a stage in his ridden career, just because he finds them easy. Use greater variety, even within a schooling session. Employ poles and raised poles for interest, and mix schooling with hacking and hill work for strengthening.

# WORK DIFFERENT MUSCLE SETS ON DIFFERENT DAYS

With any horse that is new to schooling, be it young in age or in experience, or if you intend to progress beyond basic training levels and do more work on the higher scales of training – engagement, straightness and collection – it is important to plan ahead and work different muscle sets on different days. If you work the same set two days in a row, you risk damaging muscles beyond the small amount of stress needed to build them up. Working different sets on consecutive days will also avoid muscular pain that may stress the horse and potentially sour his attitude to work. As a consequence, you will need to plan a week's worth of training sessions in order to address different aspects of training on different days.

The following are examples of weekly work plans:

## The novice horse

Day 1: School session, working on rhythm and suppleness. Choose a selection from: #1, #3, #5, #6, #7, #8, #10, #12, #13, #17, #27. Targeting the lateral bending muscles.

Day 2: Hack.

Day 3: Lunge for work with side reins and possibly over trotting poles or raised trotting poles.

Day 4: School session, working on forwardness and responses. Include a few circles and turns, but do not over-ask for bending today. Choose from #14, #15, #16, #18, #20, #28, #29, #35, #40, #61, #62. Targeting the pushing muscles.

Day 5: Hack.

Day 6: Trotting pole work and small grids. Targeting the lifting muscles.

Day 7: Day off.

With a very young horse, reduce this to no more than four days ridden work a week, including variety.

## The established horse

Day 1: School session, working on the development of engagement. Choose a selection from #22, #23, #24, #25, #26, #29, #30, #31, #41, #43, #47, #54, #55, #56, #57, #59. Targeting the carrying muscles.

Day 2: School session, working on suppleness. Choose from #12, #13, #17, #23, #24, #25, #26, #27, #32, #36, #38, #44, #52, #58, #86. Targeting the lateral bending muscles.

Day 3: Hack or pole/grid work.

Day 4: School session, working on further development of lateral work. Choose from #36, #37, #38, #49, #53, #58, #67, #68, #69, #70, #71, #72, #74, #75, #76, #77, #79 & #80. Targeting the carrying muscles.

Day 5: School session, working on transitions and medium gaits. Choose from #14, #15, #18, #28, #50, #51, #54, #56, #59, #60, #61, #62, #63, #64, #65, #66. Targeting reactions and pushing muscles.

Day 6: Hack.

Day 7: Day off.

## The advanced horse

Day 1: School session, working on strength. Choose a selection from #54, #57, #58, #59, #69, #73, #82, #83, #88, #101, #102, #103, #105, #106, also rein back to half-steps or piaffe, depending on training level. Targeting the carrying muscles.

Day 2: School session, working on developing the flying changes, #82, #89–#98. Targeting forwardness, straightness and responses.

Day 3: Hack or pole/grid work.

Day 4: School session, working on developing the zig-zags. Depending on level, choose from #52, #70, #74, #76, #77, #90, #99, #100. Developing suppleness and self-carriage.

Day 5: School session, working on developing the canter pirouettes. Choose from #17, #83, #85, #101, #102, #103, #105, #106. Targeting the carrying muscles.

Day 6: Hack.

Day 7: Day off.

## THE HORSE NEEDS TO DO WHAT HE FINDS HARD

To improve his way of going, a horse needs to do what he finds hard. By nature, a horse will be disinclined to make the effort to change, but must be guided to do so by his rider/trainer. Once he *has* made the requested effort, use what he *can* do easily as a reward, for example, finish a session with something he enjoys, such as medium trot or tempi changes.

# WARM-UP STRATEGIES

Whatever your aspirations for a schooling session – or indeed, for a competition – you should have a clear idea of an effective warm-up strategy before you begin your full work session, or do your final preparations prior to going to the competition arena.

When you start a ridden session, no matter what the horse's training level, his body needs to be prepared for work by warming-up in order to avoid the risk of physical injury to joints and muscles. Think of the synovial fluid inside his joints like engine oil – it thickens when the horse is not active, and is not as effective at lubricating the joints until it has been warmed-up, and slightly thinned. Working the horse too hard before this point risks injury. Muscles are the same – the fibres are less elastic until warmed-up, so always take the time to do a warm-up routine, and also a warm-down at the end.

## General warm-up plan

1. Stretching, exercise #32. Eight minutes in walk, five minutes in trot and canter.
2. Two minutes break to check your girth and adjust any equipment.
3. Five minutes connecting the horse. For example, exercises #1 or #3, lots of changes of direction (#4, #5, #6, #9, #11, #12), and transitions (#14, #15, #16). For more advanced horses, include some leg yielding and shoulder-in into this session.
4. Now the horse is ready to work. If your warm-up is prior to competition, take the next ten minutes for a final tune-up of movements, not forgetting to give yourself enough time for last-minute preparations, such as removing boots and getting to the competition arena!

## Warm-up in hot weather, and for non-stabled horses

To a small degree, in warm weather and for horses that are on the move in the field immediately before you ride, you can shorten the initial stretching period in walk; however, do not dispense with it entirely, as the muscles still need stretching before they are ready to work at peak efficiency.

In very hot weather, especially with chunkier-built horses that retain more body heat, shorten each phase by a few minutes and include more frequent walk breaks. For peak performance in competition, aim to do no more than twenty minutes in total, including your last-minute preparations.

## Warm-up in cold weather

Provide the horse with an exercise sheet for at least the initial fifteen minutes to keep his back and hindquarters relatively warm.

In extremely cold weather, you may need to move on into trot or canter sooner than ideal, as he may become colder rather than warmer in walk. If so, keep the gait initially quite small and relatively slow to limit potential damage to the joints.

## Warming-up a lazy horse

Once the stretching period is done, use more transitions (exercises #14, #16, #18) to put the horse on your aids, and ride predominantly long, straight lines rather than curves and circles. The open space in front of the horse will encourage forward thinking, and straight lines are less demanding of the hind legs, so that he should be more willing.

## Warming-up a tense horse

Even during the initial stretching period, use more patterns such as #6, #7, #10, #13, & #15, to help keep him focused inward, away from the external environment.

Once you start to put him together, use plenty of smaller circles and curved lines (#3, #10, #12, #21, #23) – when the horse bends, he must contract the muscles on the inside of his body, which means those on the outside must relax to allow the bend.

Also use leg yield exercises #33–#39. By crossing his hind legs, you mobilize (rock) his pelvis, which in turn loosens his back so it is able to lift and swing.

# DARE TO MAKE MISTAKES AND FEEL UNCOMFORTABLE

Schooling to improve a horse must never be about covering up training issues, even if exposing them is an uncomfortable experience (as it often will be).

In competition, riders can learn to create movements and ways of going that *look* right, without being produced in a correct way; this is one of the skills of the successful competitor. However, if that rider continues to do the same in training and is not prepared to expose underlying issues, but continues to 'paper over the cracks', at some point in their career the basic problem will prevent that horse from developing further until time is taken to put it right.

For example, a horse that leans onto the right shoulder may be presented in a test *looking* as though he is genuinely bending to the right using an indirect inside rein, with the rein held into, or even across, the withers, to push the shoulders to the outside. If this aid is also used in training, the horse will quickly learn to lean onto the rider's right hand for support, backing up the issue and perpetuating it. In putting his body weight over his right fore and using the rider's right hand as a prop, he can avoid carrying weight on his right hind leg. In other words, this also impacts his ability to engage correctly and lift himself up off his forehand.

To address this, the rider must be prepared to move the right rein away from the shoulder and attempt to bend the horse with the correct use of the right leg. At first, with his prop removed, the horse will fall inwards on corners and circles – a very uncomfortable feeling for the rider, who will want to use the indirect inside rein to upright the horse and keep him out around the curve, but he must resist doing so! This horse must be taught the correct response to the inside *leg*. When the rider's right leg is applied, he must contract his right-hand side intercostal (ribcage) muscles in order to shorten the right-hand side of his body and lengthen the left. This creates body bend. As a result of this correct use of his musculature, his right hindleg will step forward underneath his body, following in the track of his right fore, and creating the beginnings of engagement.

Exercise #17 ('Spirals') is the most useful pattern to employ for this correction. On the right rein the horse will willingly reduce the circle, as this allows him to fall inwards onto his right shoulder. The rider's challenge, then, is to enlarge the circle with use of the inside leg alone to push him outwards. If achieved correctly, the end result will be a horse that has understood to move away from the inside leg, has bent his body and achieved correct tracking, transferred some weight onto his hind legs, and connected to the outside rein. In other words, he will have formed a genuine connection from inside leg to outside rein. None of these improvements will be possible if the rider continues to use the indirect rein.

# SOMETIMES YOU MUST SACRIFICE ONE THING IN THE SHORT TERM TO ACHIEVE A REAL CHANGE IN THE OVERALL WAY OF GOING

This is another one of those places where a rider might feel uncomfortable. It is quite normal for a rider to want to maintain an aspect of the way of going that they feel is established, but sometimes it is not possible to make training progress without accepting that allowing one thing to go missing for a brief time might be the only way for the horse to gain a new understanding of something else.

An apt description of this is that it can sometimes be necessary to 'break a few eggs to make an omelette'. In other words, things might need to become messy before the final product can be created.

An example of this necessity can be found in exercise #18 ('Legs on Short Side, Legs off on Long Side'), where in the short term the rider may have to accept a temporary loss of outline in order to gain a genuine response from the horse to their leg aids. To be trainable, a horse must have a keen response to leg aids and therefore, in this case, such a response takes precedence over maintenance of the outline. Once the horse produces an acceptable response consistently, the rider can then return to addressing the matter of keeping a correctly rounded outline at the same time.

# MAKING UNCOMFORTABLE CHANGES WITHOUT HARMING THE HORSE'S CONFIDENCE

Bear in mind that in the process of the above examples it will not be just the rider who feels uncomfortable, but the horse also. By nature, horses do not embrace change; they are creatures of habit.

Because a rider sits nearer to the horse's forehand than to his hind end, an uneducated horse will tend to carry approximately 60 per cent of the combined body weight of horse and rider on their forehand, and only 40 per cent on the hindquarters. As mentioned in the introduction, one of the purposes of schooling horses is to maintain and promote their physical well-being.

This can only be achieved by training them, both in terms of their understanding of how to respond to a rider's aids and in the gradual development of their physique, until they are able to transfer more of that combined weight onto their stronger, more robust hind end – in other words, engagement, leading to collection.

Making such demands may be met with resistance, not because horses are 'difficult' or 'unwilling', but because they are innately averse to change. So many are marvellously accepting of the questions we ask them, but if a horse is resistant, the rider must always ask themselves, 'Does he really understand what is being asked of him?' and 'Is he physically capable of doing what he is being asked to do at this time?' It is the rider's responsibility to be able to honestly answer 'Yes' to both these questions before making any decision on how to proceed.

## DISTURB, THEN PRAISE

When it is necessary to disturb the horse out of his comfort zone (habit), he may become unsettled and anxious. Pushing him out of balance, asking for a quicker response, moving sideways with bigger steps – all these things (and many more) are essential for progress, but will likely cause the horse to feel nervous.

When the horse has responded in the desired fashion, *praise him immediately*. The most effective positive reinforcement has been shown to be feeding a treat, but for praise without pausing the session, use your voice and give him a scratch on the withers.

Scientific studies have shown scratching the horse on the withers (imitating allogrooming, where horses scratch each other on the withers with their lips and teeth) lowers the horse's heart rate and is more effective in relaxing the horse, rather than patting, which has no measurable effect.

## HOW LONG WILL IT TAKE TO RETRAIN (CORRECT) A FAULT?

Correcting a single training error, such as the one in the above example, may take anything from a couple of sessions to a couple of months, or in some cases even longer depending on how deeply ingrained the misunderstanding is. As mentioned already, horses are creatures of habit, and changing their habits, once formed, can be quite a challenge. This is why it is so important that such compromising aiding is used only briefly for the purposes of a competition performance, and never backed up in schooling sessions.

Each horse will improve at his own speed; this cannot be rushed. A rider or trainer needs to cultivate endless patience, while at the same time addressing training shortcomings constantly.

As a rule of thumb, taking a poorly trained horse and re-educating it fully will take approximately two years: one year to take the old training apart and one year to put the new understanding and muscle development in place. A very good incentive to get it right first time around!

## A FRIGHTENED HORSE CANNOT LEARN

Only if a horse is in a relaxed state of mind does he have the capacity to learn. However, to give him new educational experiences you will have to push him out of his comfort zone. This may well make him nervous, so once you have the reaction you requested praise him immediately, and wait for him to relax again before repeating the exercise or continuing on to another.

## COMPETING CAN BE DETRIMENTAL TO SCHOOLING

In competition, the goal is to produce a good performance. Often, to do this, a rider must ask their horse to do a transition or a movement in a specific position in the arena, even if the preparation is not satisfactory or complete. This compromises the horse's ability to respond to the rider's request, and teaches him that he does not always have to answer in a totally correct manner.

# SAMPLE WORK PLANS

# STRATEGIES TO IMPROVE SUPPLENESS

Every horse begins life with a 'stiff' side and a 'supple' side. Each presents its own challenges and needs addressing from the start of ridden work (Scale 2 – suppleness).

By nature, the muscles on one side of the body (the so-called 'stiff' side) are longer and weaker than the muscles on the 'supple' side, which are short, tight, and strong. This totally natural inequality in the two sides of the horse's body means that it is permanently bent into a slight banana shape, even when standing still.

It is important that the rider/trainer understands this to be the natural state of affairs, and not that the horse is being 'difficult' or 'resistant', so that impatience or misinterpretation do not cause a rider to use strength, gadgets or punishment in their attempts to get the horse to bend 'correctly'.

The rider's job is to carefully and gradually stretch the short, tight muscles on one side, while strengthening the long, weak ones on the other, using targeted exercises.

**Goals:** to push the horse to achieve a little more bend at each training session. It will take months to achieve big changes, so be patient, and push his boundaries just a little each time you school.

*Choose from the exercises listed in each section below – do not try to do all of them in one session.*

## The novice horse

1. Start the ridden session with a basic warm-up, as described above.

2. Once the horse is ready to work, start *on his stiffer rein* with exercise #1 – the 20m circle. Review the details of this exercise for how to address common issues, particularly that of falling in.

3. Ride a spiral (#17), only reducing the size by a little. Repeat as many times as you need until you feel some yielding of his ribcage towards the outside.

4. Once the horse has made the effort to contract his inside ribcage muscles (intercostals), which also requires him to have stretched the tight set on the outside, ride out of the pattern onto a straight line.

5. Make a change of rein. You have many options to choose from. For example, #4, #6, #7, #9, #10, #11. Within each work session vary your choice of pattern – try to ride a different one each time you change direction.

6. On the 'supple' side – the one which has the easier inside bend – ride a 20m circle, but try to keep his body and neck quite straight.

7. After using the basic large circles to supple him a little, progress to other suppling exercises:

   ❏ Loops (#8).

   ❏ Changes of direction (#6, #7, #10).

   ❏ Serpentines (#12, #13, #15 & #27).

   ❏ Add more circles, depending on the size of circle the horse can perform (#3, #21, #23 & #25).

   ❏ Through all these exercises, try to gain more bend on the 'stiff' side, and keep him straighter on the 'supple' side, making sure to control the tendency to fall onto his outside shoulder in this direction.

   ❏ Make plenty of changes of direction to give the muscles on each side a bit of a rest, while you work on the other side.

   ❏ Also include periods of free walk on a long rein at least once or twice during a session. If he performs this correctly with his head and neck lowered, before you pick him back up to a working outline, you will be developing his longitudinal (top line) suppleness as well as his lateral (bending) suppleness.

Finish the session by riding large circles in the stretched position (#32, #86).

## The established horse

1. Start with a regular warm-up to bring the horse's muscles up to working temperature.

2. Use some of the Novice horse's work programme to put him onto your aids and to begin suppling his body.

3. Once he is ready, ride smaller circles (#3, #7, #23, #24, #25, #26).

4. Start to use easy leg yield patterns to further develop his suppleness (#33, #35–#39).

5. Intersperse leg yields with small circles.

6. Make plenty of changes of direction using patterns that go directly from one curve to another, without a straight line in between (#6, #7, #8. #12, #13, #21, #26).

7. As for the novice horse, include periods of stretching at intervals throughout the session.

8. Finish the session on a figure of eight comprised of two circles of a size the horse finds relatively easy, in the stretched position (#32).

## The advanced horse

Even at advanced level, horses will always find the work easier in one direction than the other, and if not constantly monitored their bodies will revert to their old crooked defaults with surprising speed.

Addressing suppleness in the advanced horse largely involves lateral work, including ribbon exercises, where the horse is moved from one lateral movement to another, to another.

For example:

❑ During your warm-up, use counter-flexion exercises to ensure that he is supple at the poll, and with full acceptance of the bit with a relaxed jaw (#52).

❑ Move on to patterns such as leg yield zigzags (#38) and leg yield to shoulder-in (#49) for basic suppling, before starting to string more movements together.

❑ Exercises such as shoulder-in to renvers, and back to shoulder-in (#53), is suppling and at the same time engaging, and is particularly suitable for energetic horses.

❑ Other patterns such as half-pass to renvers to shoulder-in (#70), half-pass to renvers to half-pass (#71), and half-pass to leg yield to half-pass (#72) are all great suppling exercises, and you can connect them into 'ribbons', for example:

❑ From the centre line ride half-pass, to renvers, to shoulder-in (#70), then ride the short side in either shoulder-in or travers, followed by half-pass, to leg yield, to half-pass (#72) the whole way across the diagonal of the arena. Repeat on the other rein.

❑ Another example of a ribbon exercise would be to ride half-pass right from the track to the centre line, then at the centre line take the haunches into the lead (right renvers) down the centre line and turn *left*, keeping the renvers position. At the start of the long side, change the bend from renvers to shoulder-in (same position, opposite bend), and go from shoulder-in to half-pass left and repeat.

❑ The ultimate exercise is the four positions on the circle (#58), changing position and/or bend as many times as you want, until the horse feels really supple. Once this is achieved, turn away out of the circle onto the other rein, and repeat the exercises the other way around. One of the best features of this pattern is that you can choose which of the positional or bend changes has the biggest effect on the individual horse, and keep working on that until the suppleness improves.

# STRATEGIES TO IMPROVE CONTROL OF THE SHOULDERS, LEADING TOWARDS STRAIGHTNESS

Until the rider can control the horse's natural tendency to fall onto one or other shoulder according to the individual's natural crookedness, it will be impossible to develop balance and, eventually, engagement, both of which are contingent on the shoulders being directly in front of the haunches.

Although full straightness does not appear in the scales of training until scale #5, control of the shoulders should be addressed as soon as the horse and rider have enough understanding of the aids needed to move the shoulders independently of the haunches. Eventually, this will lead to straightness.

## The novice horse

- Suppling exercises are the first step – *see* the section above. The aim is to improve the equality of suppleness to both sides, so that the horse is in a position to be able to achieve the earlier straightening exercises.
- Check shoulder control by frequent riding of inside tracks (#20).

## The established horse

- Ride counter-flexion (#52).
- Ride leg yield exercises. *See* #33 for aiding corrections to control the outside shoulder.
- Also as suggested in #33, ride leg yield from the centre line towards the track and intersperse with a few steps forward in a straight line. When the outside shoulder starts to lead too much, use outside leg and rein to stop going sideways, and ride a few steps straight forward, parallel to the track. Once the horse is straight, ask for leg yield again.
- Ride a two-step leg yield zigzag (#38). This moves the shoulders from one side to the other, giving an experience of placing the shoulders independently.
- If the horse falls onto the right shoulder, practise leg yielding to the left, away from the track.
- For this same horse, also ride leg yield right from the centre line, and at the quarter line change to shoulder-out (shoulder-in right), travelling along the quarter line.

- Ride counter-canter exercises, in particular #41, sustaining the counter-canter around the entire arena. In counter-canter on the track, the horse's shoulders should be closer to the fence than the haunches, with minimal positioning of the head and neck towards the leading leg – in other words, slightly shoulder-fore towards the leading leg.

## The advanced horse

- Straightness is of ever-increasing importance as the horse progresses through the training levels. By the time the horse is advanced, the independent controls of shoulders and haunches will be established, but the rider should continue to monitor and further develop full straightness, which is essential to even loading and even use of the two hind legs. Any crookedness or inequality will show up during the more demanding exercises, in particular steep half-passes, full extensions, piaffe and passage.
- Halts are a good diagnostic at this level. Only if the contact is genuinely even in the two reins will halts be square as a result of training, and not just as a habit taught by squaring the horse up after a halt is achieved.
- All the lateral work should be monitored for unequal weight in the two reins, which is a symptom of the horse using the rider's contact for support instead of using a specific hind leg. More weight in one rein indicates the hind leg on that side is not supporting or pushing with sufficient strength.
- Transitions must always be straight, particularly walk-canter and canter-walk (#56, #82), or halt, all of which are strengthening exercises. Any evasion by deviation from correct alignment (which in canter should be a slight shoulder fore position) is an indicator of a lack of willingness to carry weight equally on both hind legs, and should be targeted for correction.
- Collection exercises, such as simple changes (#82), and those for developing canter pirouettes (#83, #101, #102), should be executed in slight shoulder-fore position, to target the weight carrying capacity of the inside hind leg.

# STRATEGIES TO DEVELOP CONNECTION TO THE OUTSIDE REIN

In the earlier stages of training your focus will be on the first two scales of training: rhythm and suppleness. As these improve, developing an elastic contact becomes possible. Once this is achieved, the horse will be ready to be 'put into the outside rein', or securely connected from 'inside leg to outside rein'.

Exercises to put the horse into the outside rein are:

1. Small circles (#3, #23, #24, #25, #26). When the horse is correctly bent (aligned) to a small circle, yield the inside rein forward for a couple of steps. If the bend remains unchanged, then the horse is connected from inside leg to outside rein. If not, try again, but press your inside leg more firmly against the horse's ribcage to create genuine bend through the body, and when the bend feels secure, check it out by again yielding the inside rein forward. Eventually you should be able to ride the entire circle with the inside rein yielded forward, steering completely with the outside rein.

2. Leg yielding. *See* in particular #33, #36, #37, #38.

3. Spirals (#17) are one of the best exercises for achieving connection. Once the spiral is completed, and there is more weight in the outside rein, continue along the outside track with a feeling that you are still pushing the horse outward, just as you did on the spiral – this is the inside leg pushing the horse towards the outside rein.

4. For tricky horses that do not connect with the easier exercises, use an adapted form of counter-flexion on a circle (#52). Once you have the horse in the outside flexion, carefully return him to an inside bend using your *inside leg* and easing the outside rein gradually forward as the bend changes. Keep some weight in the outside rein, and do not be tempted to use the inside rein – true bend must come from your inside leg. Continue to press with the inside leg against his ribcage, pushing him towards the outside rein to maintain the connection.

**With a genuine connection to the outside rein, the horse bends slightly to the inside, with a lighter inside rein contact.**

# STRATEGIES TO IMPROVE ENGAGEMENT AND COLLECTION

One of the main purposes of training a horse is to enable him to take more weight on the haunches and so reduce the amount of weight he carries on the more fragile front legs. The bonus is that this will gain you a lighter and more mobile forehand.

The dreaded comment 'on the forehand' written on so many dressage test sheets should never be treated as a criticism, but as an observation of a condition that all horses start ridden life with as a result of the rider's weight in the saddle. Even the most expensive, naturally uphill horses need to be strengthened in the right muscles and taught the techniques necessary to carry a rider without damaging themselves.

Remember the Scales of Training detailed at the front of this book? You will notice that 'engagement' and 'collection' come in the latter half of the scales. The reason for this is that unless the earlier scales (rhythm, suppleness and contact) are fairly well established, the horse and rider will not have the tools necessary to achieve the later scales. Hence why we are showing horses in lower-level dressage tests while they are still 'on the forehand'!

The tools to engage, and ultimately collect, a horse, are:

1. Smaller circles.
2. Transitions.
3. Lateral work.

Obviously, in the earlier stages of training only the first two of these are relevant.

## HOW MUSCLES ARE BUILT

To make muscles stronger, and to build more muscle, it is necessary to minutely stress the muscle fibres in order to get the body to repair them and to add new muscle mass. This tiny amount of damage causes low-grade pain – think of the muscle soreness you feel after an energetic workout. To keep the horse keen to work, avoid stressing the same muscles two days in a row.

## The novice horse

1. Once you have completed your warm-up routine, start putting the horse onto your aids by riding gradually smaller circles, taking it to the limits of what the horse can manage without losing rhythm. 15m circles (#3), 10m circles (#23), and all sizes in between can be used. While riding the circles keep the horse in the same balance – do not let him drop down in front. Do this by keeping his head and neck at the same height while asking for consistent impulsion as you travel around the circle. Circles are harder work for the horse than straight lines, and given the opportunity as they get further around a circle horses will tend to either lose impulsion (possibly slowing down), or drop onto the forehand. By keeping both energy and balance consistent around each circle, you will gain engagement.

2. Between circles add in some transitions, such as trot-walk-trot (#14), and trot-halt-trot. Ensure that you ride the hind legs under the body *with your legs on* in the downwards transitions, and ask for prompt upwards transitions that go immediately into a clear working trot, and do not 'wind up' gradually via some initial smaller steps.

3. If the horse is capable, include some baby leg yield patterns (#33, #35, #36, #39) to establish a clear inside leg to outside rein connection. Include spirals (#17), which give you both a small circle and a leg yield in the same exercise.

4. In canter, if possible ride some basic counter-canter patterns – counter-canter is an engaging exercise because, with the leading hind leg on the *outside* of the pattern, it has to travel further to remain under the horse's body, with resultant strengthening. *See* exercises #40, #41, #42 and #43.

5. Finish the session with stretching on as small circles as the horse can manage with relative ease (#32, #86).

## The established horse

This horse is no longer on the forehand, but is in a moderately horizontal balance. He will be working towards the engagement and early collection required to bring him *eventually* into an uphill way of going.

*What follows is a round-up of the exercises that can be used with a horse at this stage of development.* **DO NOT** *use all of them in the same work session.*

1. Warm-up as usual. Also use the volte with shoulder-in (#31) to fully engage his core muscles.

2. Follow the same advice as for the novice horse, but using smaller circles (#23, #24, #25, #26), sometimes alternating with larger circles (#47).

3. Use many transitions (#14, #54), either alone or interspersed between the small circles, and include rein back, which can be performed between poles (#29) or on the track, with direct transitions such as trot-halt, and halt-trot into and out of the rein back.

4. Add engaging lateral exercises, such as leg yield into a small circle (#55), lateral work which includes transitions (#50, #51, #63), shoulder-in and travers (which are engaging of themselves, (#48), renvers exercises (renvers is the most engaging position) #53, #58, #70.

5. The purpose of a pirouette is to bend the hind leg joints and lower the croup, so these should be included (#79, #80, #83, #85) at whatever stage of development the horse has achieved. Walk pirouettes are a good exercise to use when picking the horse back up again after a rest break.

6. In canter, ride many direct transitions into and out of walk (#56, #57, #59) and more advanced counter-canter patterns, such as #43 & #41 with a small half-circle. Also maintain counter-canter around deeper loops (#40), on circles of all sizes, and serpentines (#12, #27).

7. Make sure to give the horse adequate rest breaks between exercises: take the pressure off by allowing him to stretch his frame. This can be done in all three gaits, or in walk for additional aerobic recovery.

8. Also include, particularly towards the end of the session, some work in the medium gaits, to refresh his gaits and leave him with a forward-thinking memory at the end of a hard session.

9. Finish the session also using stretching on circles (#32).

## The advanced horse

By this point the horse should be sufficiently engaged to be in an uphill balance, and the work will be about increasing collection – the ability to sit and carry weight on the haunches with bent hind leg joints and a lowered croup.

Continue to use many of the exercises detailed above for the established horse, but now you can afford to push the boundaries a little further.

As for the above – *do not use all the exercises in one session,* but pick a different topic for different days. Perhaps one day work on the transitions, and another day, the canter pirouettes. Always stretch the horse (#32) in between exercises, both to allow the carrying muscles a recovery break, and to continue developing the flexibility of the frame.

1. Work at this stage of the horse's career is about mixing the use of the basic strengthening tools such as small circles and transitions, along with the more advanced lateral work and further exercises such as half-steps (#88).

2. Small circles: push the horse's boundaries in terms of circle size, always with the goal that he comes out of the circle with a more uphill carriage than he went in with (#87).

3. Transitions: these should now be clearly direct, and more extreme, such as canter to halt, and rein back to canter (#57). Always ensure in downward transitions that the horse takes approximately three increasingly collected steps before achieving the change of gait – this maximizes the strengthening benefits of each transition. Upward transitions must go directly from one gait to the next, with the steps of the new gait immediately at the regular size and speed, that is, not via a few 'winding up' steps.

4. Add work with half-steps, such as #88. They can also be employed before any corner, or indeed, anywhere around the arena once the horse understands the aids in order to develop more strength in the carrying muscles. When riding out of half-steps, always think of maintaining the uphill balance – take care not to waste the sitting effect of the half steps by allowing the shoulders to drop as you exit.

5. Lateral work: combine lateral work with transitions (#50, #51, #59, #63, #64), and increase the angle and length of half pass patterns – in the 60m arena, instead of riding from D–E, ride from F–S. Use renvers patterns (#53, #58, #70, #71), and place lateral movements on smaller circles – #58 on a smaller circle is highly engaging.

6. More of the work at this level will be in the canter, with the ultimate goal of the full canter pirouette. Develop the 'pirouette canter' using frequent transitions from collection to ultra-collection (#83), and then use a variety of patterns such as #85, #101, #102, #103, #104, #105, and #106, depending on the stage of development of the pirouette, and what suits the temperament of the horse.

7. Finish your session with stretching in rising trot on a small figure of eight (#86) to maximise the suppling of his body when his muscles are at their warmest and most pliable.

## KEEP YOUR HORSE'S ATTITUDE SWEET

When working on such concentrated collection be very aware of your horse's physical tolerance: do not continue for longer than necessary with any specific exercise. Even if you only over-tire the muscles without causing damage to them, you may make the horse sore, and reluctant to comply in future – horses have good memories, especially for pain! You do not want to destroy his joy in working with you, which is the opposite of our end goal of developing a healthy, happy athlete.

**Warming down after a work session in a relaxed, stretched outline.**

# STRATEGIES TO DEVELOP AND IMPROVE MEDIUM GAITS

### Pre-requisites for medium gaits

To be able to perform medium gaits, some degree of engagement is essential, so that the horse is accustomed to bringing his hind legs forward under his body, where he will need them to develop the required push for the bigger strides, and to maintain some balance. *Do not* start working on mediums before the horse has a correct response to the half-halt, so that his balance is not too far onto his shoulders when asked to lengthen.

It is also essential to understand the aiding necessary to create medium gaits.

1. Impulsion is essential for medium gaits, and must be created *before* you ask for the medium. The rider's legs create impulsion during the preparatory steps. *Do not use your legs during the medium* – hammering your legs against the horse's ribcage will only cause him to tighten his muscles, which will shorten his strides, not lengthen them.

2. The rider's *seat* is responsible for the length of stride – use a bigger, longer swing of the pelvis (in rising or sitting), while remaining in the *same speed and rhythm*.

3. Your hands must move slightly forward to permit the horse's frame to lengthen a little, but do not lose contact.

4. The return to the working (or collected) gait is achieved by reducing the size of your seat action and re-applying your legs to bring the horse's hind legs forward under his body.

### The novice horse

1. Discover which of the exercises works best for the individual horse: for the lazier horse use #61, so you do not have starting and stopping to discourage forwardness. For the horse that falls onto the forehand, use #60 and #62, just working on the transitions until he can sustain the medium gradually for a step or two longer each time.

2. Initially, develop the mediums using the track, rather than the diagonals of the arena. The horse derives psychological support from the track, and will tend to find it easier to keep his balance alongside a fence or a wall. This helps with the confidence he needs to take the bigger strides.

3. Some horses can be persuaded to take bigger strides more easily on a circle, which again helps with the maintenance of balance, because the inside hind leg comes further forward underneath the body as a result of the bend. This is especially so with medium canter.

4. In trot, try combining a few exercises. For example: ride a zigzag leg yield (#38) for one long side between the track and the quarter line to loosen his shoulders. At C (or A), ride a 15m circle (#3) or a 10m circle (#23) to gather his hind legs underneath him, and then go forward to medium either on the long side, or the diagonal, depending on his confidence.

### The established horse

1. Once the horse can sustain medium strides for more than just a few steps, it is time to introduce the concept of transitions into and out of medium gaits. Work on reactions, using direct transitions (#54) around the arena to improve his strength and speed of response, and also include transitions *within* the gaits as well as between them (#62).

2. Use small circles (#60), and lateral work (#63 & #64) in preparation, so increasing the degree of engagement and/or collection prior to the medium.

3. Work on the transitions back using lateral work (#63) and repetitive patterns (#65). These are also useful for teaching riders how to ride the transitions back from medium to working/collected, because they teach the rider to ride forward into the downward transition, and not to pull back.

4. #66 may be useful with some horses, but should be used only by experienced riders.

# STRATEGIES TO INTRODUCE, DEVELOP, AND IMPROVE HALF-PASS

Of all the lateral movements, half-pass is the one that is the biggest challenge for the majority of horses (and riders) to learn. It can only be ridden successfully when the horse has sufficient collection to carry himself sideways with his weight on his hindquarters, rather than attempting to drag himself sideways with his front legs and his weight on his shoulders. Many riders attempt to teach half-pass before the necessary degree of collection is achieved, and as a consequence, much pulling, shoving, and use of inappropriate strength on the part of the rider is too often seen.

The following sequence of exercises lead up to the successful development of half-pass. Immediately the horse/rider hits a problem with half-pass, they should go back to the beginning and run through these exercises in order, until they identify the training area that needs attention, before attempting to ride the finished movement again.

1. In addition to a degree of collection, before attempting half-pass in either trot or canter, the horse must be able to perform a decent travers. If the horse struggles to achieve the necessary bend in travers, he is not yet ready to attempt half-pass. Work on suppling exercises – *see* the exercises listed in the above section for suppling established and advanced horses.

2. In travers, the horse should be able to look directly along the track at the same time as travelling with his hindquarters displaced inwards at the correct angle to the track (four tracks). This should be achieved as a result of genuine body bend, and not neck bend alone.

3. Work on increasing the angle of the travers while keeping the head and neck aligned with the track. This can be done in walk, trot and canter.

4. If there is a loss of impulsion, ride forward to a more energetic gait, and then half-halt before repositioning. Only if the hind legs are carrying the body weight can the horse successfully bend and travel sideways at the same time.

5. Alternate shoulder-in and travers (#75, which can be performed in walk and trot, as well as in canter). At first, a small circle can be placed between the two movements for bend and engagement purposes, but the horse should be able to move easily and directly between the two positions before attempting half-pass.

6. You can use the four position circle (#58) to develop the horse's flexibility, manoeuvrability and engagement further.

7. Ride travers on a diagonal line across the arena. Use poles as a guideline at first (#68).

8. Gradually increase the bend around the inside leg whilst riding this diagonally placed travers. Eventually this will become a half-pass.

9. Once you dispense with the poles, it is easier for the horse to half-pass from the centre line to the track, for example, From D to B (long arena), because you can ride a 10m half-circle onto the centre line to develop bend, and the horse will be psychologically drawn towards the track.

10. Only when the horse finds this easy should you start riding half-pass from the track to the centre line, always starting from a small position of shoulder-fore (#69) to ensure the shoulders are in advance of the quarters.

Always ride your half-pass **forward:** half-pass is a forward/sideways movement – note the order of words. Always position so that both you and the horse are looking towards the letter where you intend to arrive, and ride forwards towards it, and not just sideways. The horse cannot travel sideways if you push his haunches into the lead.

# STRATEGIES TO INTRODUCE CANTER PIROUETTES

Provided a horse is physically strong in the haunches and the back muscles, working canter pirouettes can be introduced well before the horse achieves an advanced level of training, while he is still in the developmental stage.

The following is a guideline to the order in which to introduce these patterns but, as usual, different exercises will suit different horses according to individual temperament and physical ability, so play around with the following and discover which ones work best. Eventually, the horse should be able to perform all of these patterns with relative ease, but the order in which they achieve them may vary.

Pattern #83: Repeated canter collections over the centre line. This exercise is designed to help develop the rider's ability to collect the horse from the seat without using strong half halts that might block the energy from the hindlegs. The goal is to eventually produce 'pirouette canter' at each crossing of the centre line, with the horse cantering *almost* on the spot for two to three steps before being allowed to go forward to a normal collected canter again. The repetitive nature of the exercise promotes anticipation as a means of getting the horse to 'help' the rider, by

## THE TRAINING VALUE OF CANTER PIROUETTES

The purpose of a pirouette is to teach the horse to bend all the hind leg joints – hip, stifle, hock and fetlock – in order to lower the croup. Lowering the croup is an essential component in engagement, collection, and self-carriage. As such, pirouette is a good example of how the training exercises we use are designed to improve the horse's way of going, and are not simply a movement to be performed in a dressage test.

performing the collection with smaller and smaller aiding.

Pattern #85: Working pirouette from a spiral. Spirals are an exercise every horse should learn from an early stage of their training (#17), so this is simply an extension of an already familiar exercise. The goal is that once the haunches have been displaced inward on the small circle, to feel for when the croup lowers, stay for three or four steps and then return to the large circle, possibly followed by medium canter on the circle to refresh the canter before repeating. By only asking the horse to sit to this degree for a few steps, he should not feel over-faced. For the horse that offers to sit too much, this is also a good pattern because he will not be permitted to dwell and get 'stuck'.

Pattern #79: Walk pirouettes on a square. Use this to gain a feel for the exercise, and a reminder of the aiding, with the next step being to replicate it in canter.

Pattern #101: Quarter canter pirouettes on the square. At first, ride a quarter pirouette on alternate corners, riding the intervening corners as simple turns. Once this becomes easy, ride a quarter pirouette on every corner. Pay particular attention to coming out of each quarter pirouette on to the desired straight line, and not permitting the horse to over-turn.

Pattern #104: The 'V' shape. This is also a quarter pirouette, but ridden off a diagonal line and with a fast depart, instilling in the horse the knowledge that he must leave the 'sitting' position of the pirouette with energy. This can be ridden on any diagonal line within the arena.

Pattern #105: Canter half pass to working pirouette. This is a fluent, continuous exercise for further strength building.

Pattern #102: Serpentine with canter working half pirouettes. From here on, as the horse becomes stronger and performs the working pirouettes with increasing ease, they can gradually be reduced in size until they become the finished movement.

# IN CONCLUSION

Remember that training is a journey – you will never stop learning.

The above are some sample strategies and pattern suggestions, but are by no means exhaustive. There are other books on the topic, and in addition to working with your own trainer one of the best ways to increase your catalogue of exercises is to watch other people's lessons, and attend demonstrations and master classes with top riders and trainers.

I hope this book has provided plenty of food for thought, some new exercises for you to try, and some guidance on how schooling programmes should be structured to benefit the horse's development and well-being, from the earliest stages through to the more advanced.

More detail on the aiding system described in the text can be found in my earlier book, *The Building Blocks of Training*, with visual examples and posts on topics surrounding horse training on my website, www.debbylush.co.uk

**The ultimate goal of schooling is to create a relaxed, happy partnership.**